9.23.22

John Fisher and Thomas More

AMDG,

Bob
Conn

JOHN FISHER AND THOMAS MORE

Keeping Their Souls While Losing Their Heads

Robert J. Conrad Jr.

TAN Books
Gastonia, North Carolina

Cover design by Caroline Green

Cover images: Portrait of Saint Thomas More, painting by unknown Lombard author (17th century), © Veneranda Biblioteca Ambrosiana/Mondadori Portfolio / Bridgeman Images. Portrait of John Fisher, Bishop of Rochester, mid-16th century (oil on panel), Holbein the Younger, Hans (1497/8-1543) (follower of) / Germa, Photo © Philip Mould Ltd, London / Bridgeman Images.

Library of Congress Control Number: 2021933062

ISBN: 978-1-5051-1849-0
Kindle ISBN: 978-1-5051-1850-6
ePUB ISBN: 978-1-5051-1851-3

Published in the United States by
TAN Books
PO Box 269
Gastonia, NC 28053
www.TANBooks.com

Printed in the United States of America

To my good friends KTK and RMG

Contents

Foreword

The remarkable John Fisher entered Cambridge at the age of fourteen; he was ordained a priest in 1491 at the age of twenty-two. Ten years later, he became vice chancellor, rising to chancellor of his beloved university in 1504. The same year, he was named the bishop of Rochester. He would be confessor to the mother of King Henry VII, and possibly also a tutor to the prince who would become Henry VIII—and order his execution.

Thomas More would become a distinguished figure in all branches of the English government of Henry VIII, rising finally to the highest executive position in the realm as lord chancellor. Still, he would be warned that "the wrath of the king is death." To which he responded, "Is that all my lord? Then in good faith, there is no more difference between your grace and me, but that I shall die today and you tomorrow." There is a rich story to be told about Fisher and More, but that one line offers an entry into the story that may prefigure everything else. For it enlightens the reader to understand just what there was in the moral formation of these men that made them willing to court death in response to a prince they had served, and go with serenity to their executions.

Of the legend of Thomas More so much has been heard, but far less attention has been given to Fisher. And yet Fisher's story reveals a record of courage and conviction not any shade less than that of More's. For they shared the same depth of faith that alone could explain why both men were able to move even cheerily to their executions. Their two stories are recalled now and woven together in the most telling way by Robert Conrad in this new book—and caught so aptly in his subtitle: *Keeping Their Souls While Losing Their Heads*. More remarked to the jurors who convicted him that "we may yet hereafter in heaven merrily all meet together to our everlasting salvation." Later, he kissed his executioner and said, "Thou will give me this day greater benefit than ever any mortal man can be able to give me." For his part, Fisher prepared calmly for his execution, he dressed in his finest clothes and told his servant that this was his marriage day, and it behooved him "to dress for the solemnity of the marriage."

These stories offer a dramatic mix of law and theology, and Conrad brings to it the eye of a former federal prosecutor, now a senior federal judge in North Carolina. But he brings also the angle of a serious Catholic who takes his faith seriously, that same faith that removed from these saints the fear of death. The trials through which More and Fisher passed would not exactly pass a demanding test of "due process of law" in our own time. But Conrad leads us through the thicket.

For Fisher it began with Henry's move to divorce himself from his first wife, Catherine of Aragon. A hearing was held at the Legatine Court, and Bishop Fisher served as counsel to the queen. When Catherine stood on her own to make her case, it was simple, powerful, and affecting. She had borne his children, including three sons who had died, and she asserted that at the time of their marriage, "I was a true maid without touch of man." She pointed out that his father, King Henry VII, and her father, King Ferdinand of Spain, famous as "wise and excellent counselors," believed the marriage was "good and lawful." And finally, she reminded Henry that the pope had issued a bull confirming her marriage to be valid.

Even a gathering of tamed bishops could be chastened. Nevertheless, the fix was in. Henry declared that the bishops unanimously accepted his case, and the archbishop of Canterbury chimed in that "all my brethren here present will affirm the same." But the moment was quickly broken when Bishop Fisher said, with firmness, "No sir, not I. You have not my consent thereto." This simple but powerful response set him on the path to his execution.

More and Fisher refused to take the oaths confirming Henry's divorce, or to endorse the Act of Supremacy, establishing Henry as the Supreme Head of what was now the "Church of England." More and Fisher fell back on the understanding in the law that silence implies consent. They made a claim to "conscience" as a way of showing the want of "malice" that was necessary to the crime. But silence, of course, would not do, and so the Act of Succession took their refusal to take the oath as the "misprision of a felony." The refusal to take the oath would be regarded as a gesture of intransigence, and taken then itself as evidence enough to warrant imprisonment. Henry could not find his position settled and secure unless Fisher and More would be avowedly with him—that they would speak the telling words that cleared the air of moral doubt.

It is worth pausing to recall the sequence of legal measures brought forth by Henry and his willing aides. The first Act of Succession in March 1534 prohibited any malicious slandering by writing, print, deed, or act of the king's title. This act was followed by an oath of allegiance not only to the succession but also to the legitimacy of the king's marriage to Anne Bolyen—and the illegitimacy, then, of his prior marriage to Catherine. The Act of Supremacy made the king the "only Head of the Church of England on Earth so far as the Law of God allows." And the Treason Act that followed made it treason, punishable by death, to challenge the Act of Supremacy.

Fisher and More had held back in decorous silence from taking the oath to support Henry's divorce, and they refused to acknowledge the king as the Supreme Head of the Church. For refusing to take the oath following the Act of Succession, they were "attainted" in different bills. That is, they would be proclaimed guilty, by name, in an Act of Parliament, without one of those vexing trials that could test in a demanding way the guilt or innocence of these men—and the statute under which they were imprisoned for life.

More and Fisher would fall back, even in their own minds, on the "claims of conscience." But the notion of conscience has been the parent of serious confusion in this story. The most famous account of More has come through Robert Bolt's play-turned-movie *A Man for All Seasons*. Bolt had More say that what matters to him is not that "I *believe*" these arguments to be true, but that "*I* believe" them. In the vernacular of our day, Bolt sought to show that the lodestar for More was to be comfortable *with himself.* That stands in striking contrast to John Paul II's teaching that our conscience is directed to an objective set of moral norms outside ourselves. And as Conrad shows, that is the only account of More that makes sense. For Bolt, the key to More was the "possession of self"—that More was a "hero of selfhood." To take that path, as John Paul II said, was to move to a "subjectivist" understanding, and in that way, "the inescapable truths disappear." Conrad catches the core of the matter: "[More and Fisher] were not adamantine followers of self-will but servants of the one true God who spoke through his Word and his Church. Their shared conviction was that . . . God was truth, and that his Church was a truth-telling institution."

As my late teacher Leo Strauss used to say, it is critical to try to understand a writer as he understands himself. It is evident that Robert Conrad sees the lessons of Fisher and More as offering, as he says, a "script" for our lives. And he sees his whole life bound up in the lessons he is trying to glean—not merely in his role as a prosecutor and judge, but as husband and father. But there is yet something more: his friends know that he was also a legendary figure in college basketball in his years at Clemson. Thus, he brings to the story also the lens of a man who has been closely attentive to the grace and character so often tested in sports. But then he does a turn, using the analogy of a modern sport, golf, to illuminate a key point in Fisher's teaching. Our friends doing what is called the New Natural Law will write about the fascination for the drama and grace of a game as one of the most natural "goods" to which human beings are readily drawn—as with the good of falling in love. People don't ask, "Why did you fall in love?" And for similar reasons, the question of why people are drawn to an exciting game, played at a high level, is something that needs no auxiliary motive to explain. It explains itself. Some critics have wondered, though, whether these felt goods are put on the same plane, or whether the devotion to God must be a good rising above the rest. But others will say that there is no conflict among the motives: the grace and character manifested in sports may offer an understanding that guides the rest of one's life. The pressing question of, "What is the purpose of the game?" leads naturally to the question, "What is the purpose of *my life*?" Conrad recalls a football star in Chicago where he and I grew up who, after a mesmerizing career, wrote a memoir called *I Am Third*. Clearly, he understood where his celebration in the public arena stood in the hierarchy of things. He suffered no confusion about the ordering of goods. First came God, second the family, then he came third. In his own natural way, as Conrad sees it, this athlete grasped the same ordering of ends that commanded the devotions of Thomas More and carried him to his death, without a trace of moral doubt.

But anyone who knows Robert Conrad knows that his own life has been connected in the same way. He has cultivated a lovely family, vibrant and reverent, sprung from the matchless Ann; they have coached their children in sports and guided them as they've grown, and they can see now the men and women they have shaped, with a loving hand, as devoted Catholics. And everything has been ordered to the rightful ranking of ends. Conrad sees Fisher and More as providing "ultimately a script for my children, and grandchildren, of the kind of man their father and grandfather longs to be." With this book, Robert Conrad gives us an account of Fisher and More that runs to the core, and with that, he invites us into the world that he and Ann have lived.

Hadley Arkes
March 19, 2021
The Feast of Saint Joseph

Introduction

In the history of England, no one looms larger than the Tudor monarch Henry VIII. He came to the throne in the first decade of the sixteenth century, a time of hope and relative peace. Initially considered the "model Renaissance prince," he was handsome, debonair, multi-lingual, athletic, and pious. In fact, he was accorded the title "Defender of the Faith" for his religious writings.

Tragically, the arc of his reign would pivot to destruction. Surrounded by sycophants, driven by an obsessive desire for a male heir, and unable to restrain his sexual appetite, he veered ineluctably into despotism. His will was imposed on everyone, in every way. He taxed his country incessantly to support wars of aggression. He married six wives, impregnating his second before divorcing the first, and marrying the third the day after executing the second. His lust for sex was matched by his lust for power, "solving" the centuries-old problem of Church and State by declaring himself head of both. Where once an itinerant preacher rose to fame by preaching, among other things, that his followers should render to Caesar that which belongs to Caesar, Henry declared his intention to make all things his.

The story in outline is well-known. When the future King Henry VIII was a boy of eight, a teenage Catherine of Aragon was married by proxy to Henry's fourteen-year-old brother, Arthur. A few years later, Catherine, then sixteen, arrived in England and was married in person. Five months later, Arthur died.

It was generally believed at the time that Arthur died leaving Catherine a virgin, "a true maid without touch of man."[1] Eight years later, Henry VIII succeeded his father as king of England. In one of his first acts, he married Catherine of his own volition. A papal bull was sought and obtained removing any impediment to the marriage based upon a potential consummation of the previous one.

Catherine conceived and bore several children, including three sons. Sadly, all but one daughter was stillborn or died within weeks. Eighteen years passed with no male heir, no one getting any younger, and an impatient potentate frustrated by the lack of an heir. Complicating matters, Henry fell in love with Anne Boleyn, the sister of a woman with whom he previously had an affair. Described by one More scholar as "an expert in the game of love,"[2] Anne required a ring and a crown before submitting to the lusty king. Unable to resist Anne's allures, he became obsessed with his "great matter"—that is, the obtaining of a divorce from Catherine in order to marry Anne Boleyn. As Shakespeare intoned in the play *Henry VIII*, Henry's "conscience had crept too near another lady."[3] This is where things stood at the beginning of matters that matter most in this book.

Entering this royal web of intrigue were two men: John and Thomas. Their integrity, courage, and good cheer would stand down Henry's regal assault upon their right to think, to practice their faith, even to live. For after a lengthy period of study, each in his own way opposed the king's divorce. At the zenith of Henry's demand for assent to his divorce, these two men asserted a resolute no.

John Fisher and Thomas More lived their lives and boldly went to their deaths refusing to capitulate to the wrath of a king in matters of faith. History remembers them well. The Catholic Church, which they died to defend, joins the Anglican Church—whose titular head, Henry VIII, presumed to assume—in considering them saints and friends of God. And outside Church circles, they are universally recognized as stalwart men of conscience.

Thomas More is the better known of the two. Considered by some as "the Father of English prose," it should come as no surprise that the English dictionary bears his influence. His declaration at the moment of death—"I die the king's good servant, and God's first"—is far better known than all of Henry's quips, proclamations, and statements put together. A More contemporary, Robert Whittington, was the first to call him "a man for all seasons." Four centuries later, another Robert, Robert Bolt, would borrow that name for his famous play. Whittington wrote, "More is a man of an angel's wit and singular learning. He is a man of many excellent virtues; I know not his fellow. For where is the man (in whom is so many goodly virtues) of that gentleness, lowliness, and affability? And as time requires, a man of marvelous mirth and pastimes and sometime of steadfast gravity—a man for all seasons."[4]

Samuel Johnson, the great eighteenth-century English moralist, said, "He was the person of the greatest virtue these islands ever produced."[5] In the preface to his book *Ecclesiastes*, Erasmus, the great Dutch philosopher and priest, lamented the loss (to execution) "of the Bishop of Rochester (Fisher) and of Thomas More, whose heart was whiter than snow, a genius such as England never had before, nor will have again."[6] Historian Hugh Trevor-Roper described him as "the most saintly of humanists (and) the most human of saints." G. K. Chesterton, nearly four hundred years after More's death and six years before his canonization in 1935, prophetically remarked, "Blessed Thomas More is more important at this moment than at any moment since his death, even perhaps the great moment of his dying; but he is not quite so important as he will be in a hundred years."[7]

John Fisher was and remains less known. Unlike More, he had no sound bite last phrase, no playwright to celebrate his virtues. Indeed, the opposite is true. In the wake of his execution, King Henry's men conducted a "campaign to obliterate his memory" by breaking up his private library,[8] burning his printed works, destroying every monument or statue of him, and removing all reference to him from St. John's College, which he founded.

But make no mistake, Fisher was acknowledged as a great man, and the greatest preacher of his day. In response to Fisher's courageous stand against him in his "great matter," Henry pretended to dismiss him, saying, "You are but one man." But long before that, Henry bragged that "no other prince had in his realm a bishop so endowed with virtue and learning."[9] Erasmus described him as "a man of incomparable holiness and knowledge." More's assessment of Fisher was that for virtue and learning, there was "no superior among living men." He praised Fisher as a man "illustrious not only by the vastness of his erudition, but much more so by the purity of his life." Fisher's first and anonymous biographer, in his work *The Early Life*, referred to him as "the very mirror and lantern of light." Virtue and learning, it seems, defined John Fisher.

It stands to reason that by dint of personality, Fisher might pale in comparison to More. Fisher was the ascetic, More the aesthete. Where More was outgoing and social, Fisher was austere. One can easily see More holding court in Parliament, in council, and at home. One cannot see Fisher engaging in small talk. He was a churchman, not a celebrated man of public life. Where More was convivial, Fisher was introverted. Where More boasted of a large family (four of his own children, one adopted step-daughter by marriage, one adopted step-daughter by love, and a foster child rescued from an abusive home), Fisher was celibate, scholarly, and reclusive. Diverse in personality, vocation, and style, they were united in their love for God. Romans 12 describes these fraternal twins: "For as in one body we have many members, and all the members do not all have the same function, so we, though many, are one body in Christ, and individually members one of another" (vv. 4–5). Viewed together, these diverse men share a common legacy of steadfast conscience, unwavering commitment to Church, and an unshakable defense of marriage.

This book is written by a Catholic layman, father, grandfather, youth coach, lawyer, former federal prosecutor, and current judge. In the course of his legal career, he deposed a president and vice president of the United States, investigated organized crime and other criminal organizations, sought and imposed the death penalty in heinous murder cases, and presided over trials with millions of dollars at stake. Yet none of these encounters compares to the study of these lives. Fisher and More suffered intense persecution and emerged smiling. They laughed at death and now, if they were right, live more splendidly than the king of England. What is the source of their joy? How can their defeat be perceived as the greatest win? Who are these guys?

I have spent an adult lifetime marveling at their witness to truth, integrity, courage, and humor. The personal inspiration received from them has resulted in a desire to share their stories. Although intimidated by their intellectual prowess, daunted by their courage, and at times bewildered by their humor in the face of adversity of the highest magnitude, I have come away invigorated, even emboldened, in my attempt to live virtuously and to increase in learning.[10]

Contemplation of their joy in the midst of adversity has reminded me of the one who said "in this world you will have tribulation" but also promised that he has overcome the world. More and Fisher were men of good cheer, overcomers. They rejoiced and were glad to suffer the rebuke, the insults, and the persecution even unto death of this world, for they knew in the next their reward would be great. They knew. And because they knew, they stood defiantly, respectfully, ultimately successfully against all the power of the king.

How to live as they lived, how to even *want* to live as they lived, is what this book is all about. It eschews a chronological narrative in exchange for a series of life stories from which lessons may be absorbed and, God-willing, applied. Lessons such as detachment from the things, even good things, of this life, courage to stand your ground, prioritizing the things of God over that of earth, and trusting that there is a King greater than the greatest king on earth. And that King loves you.

I write, purposely, about the two together. The Lord in all ages seems to have sent his friends out "two by two."[11] They worked quite differently for a common end—the one a lawyer's lawyer, the other a scholar priest. Their faithful witness, spiritual focus, and secular battle complement each other. Despite their different natures, these friends made even the loneliness of the prison tower palatable. Their united witness speaks powerfully to our world which struggles with ribaldry and turmoil not unlike that of the sixteenth century. That century, as ours, was marked by plagues, viruses, social upheaval, fears of collusion, fractious political hearings, warring religious claims, rioting, looting, and destruction of monuments. These friends point us to something better—better here and a better hereafter. Their stories warrant a common tale.

As a trial attorney and as a grandfather, I know the power that well-told stories possess to communicate truth. This book is a collection of stories of two men. More is indeed a man for all seasons, and his friend John Fisher is a man of faith and all reason. They demonstrate by their lives, and yes, especially by their deaths, that man is made for God and God is there for man. Here is a sampling of their life stories to guide, to inspire, and to emulate.

Finally, it came to me late, as my desire to write this book began to crystalize, that I had found in the lives of these men the man I wanted to be. It is obvious to all who know me that there is a considerable gap between us. And yet, More's and Fisher's sanctity, learning, and courage beckon one forward. And in the end, though Fisher was but one man, and though More died alone—separated from all whom he loved—they, each of them, knew they were leaving a script of faith, hope, and love for their families and for generations unborn. This little book is ultimately a script for my children and grandchildren of the kind of man their father and grandfather longs to be.

I will close this introduction with the words of one who has studied John Fisher more than most and reduced his thoughts into a lovely biography, whose opening salvo applies equally to Thomas More: "Dear Reader! You are about to take part in perhaps the greatest tragedy of an age that wrote Hamlet and Macbeth. Greater even than the writer's part will be yours, the reader's and the hearer's part. Only your hearing ear and your seeking eye will bring the tragedy to its own. But your seeing eye and your hearing ear must first recognize that a greater than Hamlet or Macbeth is here. They are but splendid fiction."[12]

Let us turn the page with ears to hear and eyes to see.

CHAPTER I

Conscience

"For it was much against my conscience."

The nation's capital roiled with controversy. A hearing affecting national interest was hurriedly scheduled to resolve the question of a person's qualifications for high office. During the hearing, sporadic outbursts threatened to derail the entire inquiry. A question arose, almost impossible to answer, about the sexual conduct of one of the parties nearly three decades ago. Inquisitors demanded graphic details about teenage sexual activity. Although not primarily at issue, hovering in the background were important concerns about church-state relationships, reproductive health, and the nature of marriage.

The drama could not be more pronounced, the atmosphere more electric. It seemed as if the culture of Western civilization hung in the balance.

The reference point here is not the confirmation hearing of Justice Brett Kavanaugh in 2018. It is, rather, the papal legate hearing in sixteenth-century England during the reign of Henry VIII. Admittedly, a round-about way of getting to the core principle motivating the action of More and

9

Fisher—that of conscience—it is but one of many points of comparison between sixteenth- and twenty-first-century controversies.

The question before the legatine commission was whether King Henry VIII's marriage to Catherine of Aragon was licit. Will the queen remain the king's wife? Or will the king be allowed to divorce her and marry another? Queen Catherine denies that decades ago her marriage to the king's then fifteen-year-old older brother Arthur had been consummated. The king has hearsay witnesses ready to say that it was. This question is important because of the biblical implications then thought to apply.

Henry VIII claimed to have theological scruples arising from the Levitical prohibition against marrying his brother's wife.[13] If the marriage was not consummated, then the Levitical prohibition was not operative. But even that aside, it seems no such scruple existed at the time of Henry's proposal to Catherine. The couple even sought and obtained a papal bull removing any potential impediment, then lived together relatively amicably for eighteen years. But the failure of a male heir, and perhaps his attraction to Anne Boleyn, seems to substantiate the king's scruples. God was punishing him for living in sin.

The queen's side contends a valid marriage to Henry VIII exists because her marriage to Arthur was never consummated, and pleading in the alternative like any good advocate, even if it was consummated, the papal dispensation sought and received by the royal couple at the time of their marriage dispelled any impediment.

The year is 1529. Later that year, Thomas More will be named Lord Chancellor of England. He is not yet in Henry's crosshairs. John Fisher, however, is about to place himself front and center in the king's line of sight. As counsel to the queen, Fisher attends the Legatine Court hearings held in the Great Hall of the Blackfriars in London. There, a papal commission was authorized to conduct a joint inquiry and to come to a decision based on the evidence submitted on the question of the king's marriage, and to give its verdict fast for that was the wish of the king, the result all but guaranteed. The papal legates, Cardinal Lorenzo Campeggia and Cardinal Thomas Wolsey are indebted to Henry. Campeggia was the beneficiary of the king's generosity a decade before when the see of Salisbury was bestowed upon him. And Wolsey knew "his very survival as a public figure, would depend entirely on his ability to persuade the papal curia to serve the interests of the English crown."[14] Anne Boleyn, the putative third party beneficiary of the hearings, had even written to thank Wolsey for his efforts and expressed hope that the legate matter would soon conclude "so that she could reward the Cardinal for his services."[15]

The fix was in, as described by Michael Macklem in one of the most riveting biographical chapters ever written.[16] In the great hall, there were two chairs for the legates covered with golden cloths. The floor was covered with carpets and the walls hung with tapestries. On the legates' right there was hung a cloth of estate behind a chair covered with rich tissue for the king, and on their left, a chair for the queen. Her counsel, Bishop Fisher, sat nearby.

The crier calls out, "King Harry of England come into the court"; to which the king responds, "Here my lords." The crier again, "Catherine Queen of England come into the court." To this, she made no answer but instead rose, crossed the floor, knelt down at her husband's feet, and gave one of the most powerful opening statements in English history. She:

- demanded justice from the head of justice within the realm;
- vouched that she had been a "true, humble and obedient" wife for twenty years;
- stated that she had loved those whom he had loved for his sake whether they were her natural friends or enemies;
- bore his children, including a surviving daughter, and three sons who through no fault of her own did not survive;
- asserted her virginity at the time of their marriage: "I was a true maid without touch of man";
- pointed out that his father, King Henry VII, also known as the "Second Solomon," and her father, King Ferdinand of Spain, with their "wise and excellent counselors" in both realms, believed the marriage was "good and lawful";
- reminded the king that the pope at their request had issued a bull declaring the marriage valid.

And finally, she committed her cause to God, stood up, walked out, and was gone.

Macklem concludes, "Catherine made an extraordinary impression on everyone who saw and heard her. Her simple assertion of human dignity and human worth made the proceedings of the court seem suddenly sordid and shameful."[17]

The king found himself in an unusual position—on defense. Believing the best defense to be a good offense, he made an effort to recover his position. He told the court that his scruples first arose during the discussion of a possible proposal between his three-year-old daughter Mary and the dauphine of France, and how her pedigree had been called into question. It "pricked" his conscience, he said, "pricked, vexed and troubled his mind"—on behalf of England of course—no word of Anne Boleyn. And concerned for this "noble realm," he had begun to wonder whether he might take another wife in case his "copulation with this gentlewoman were not lawful." Not for any notion of "carnal concupiscence," but for the realm.

King Henry told the legates that he had placed his doubts before all the bishops of the realm. And you know what? Not one of them disagreed. The king: "And so I did of all you, my lords, to the which you have all granted by writing under all your seals, the which I have here to show [holding up the affidavits]." The archbishop of Canterbury responds, "That is truth if it please your highness. I doubt not but all my brethren here present will affirm the same."[18]

There was a pause while the king waited for the unspoken assent of the bishops. In the silence, however, one voice rang out clearly from the queen's benches: "No, sir, not I. You have not my consent thereto."[19]

The king turned on Bishop Fisher in anger and showed him an affidavit with seals. "Look here upon this, is not this your hand and seal?"

"No, forsooth, sir, it is not my hand nor seal," Fisher answered confidently.

The king then wheeled around on the archbishop of Canterbury. "Sir, how say you? Is it not his hand and seal?"

The archbishop looks down hesitantly, then confirms the king's speculation, only to be confronted by Bishop Fisher. "That is not so, for indeed you were in hand with me to have both my hand and seal, as other of my lords had already done, but then I said to you that I would never consent to no such act for it were much against my conscience, nor my hand and seal should never be seen at any such instrument (God willing)."[20]

The archbishop, looking for a way out, counters, "You say truth, such words you had unto me, but at the last you were fully persuaded that I should for you subscribe your name and put to a seal myself, and you would allow the same."

But Fisher confronts all the power in the room assembled against him and without flinching, says, "All which words and matter under your correction, my lord, and supportation of this noble audience, there is nothing more untrue."[21]

The tension in the great hall was palpable. The archbishop did not attempt to answer. Nor did the king attempt to defend him. Instead, he passed the matter over with what amounted to an admission of the truth of what Fisher had said: "It shall make no matter. We will not stand with you in argument herein, for you are but one man."[22]

"*For you are but one man.*"

This testimony, played out in the legatine court, foreshadows the exhilarating courtroom drama of our day. Attorneys plan their strategies, prepare their affidavits, rehearse their scripts; and then, witnesses are called and testify, and everything changes. The queen impresses, the king dissembles, and the certain outcome is cast into doubt. It is riveting. Counsel for the queen, against all odds, steals victory from the jaws of defeat. The hand-chosen papal legates would rule against Henry. In words signaling this adverse ruling to the king, Cardinal Campeggio would eventually conclude:

> I come not so far to please any man . . . for fear, need, or favor, be he King or any other potentate. I have no such respect to the persons such that I will offend my conscience. I will not for favor or displeasure of any high estate or mighty prince do that thing that should be against the law of God. I am an old man, both sick and impotent, looking daily for death. What should it then avail me to put my soul in the danger of God's displeasure to my utter damnation for the favor of any prince or high estate in the world? My coming and being here is only to see justice ministered according to my conscience, as I thought thereby matter good or bad.[23]

With the conscience-inspired-courage of her counsel, Bishop Fisher, the queen temporarily prevails. The king would have to take other steps to have his way, and to have his way with Anne Boleyn.

As exciting as these courtroom-like performances are to a trial lawyer, it is obvious that much more is at play here than the competitive excitement of legal advocacy.

One can well envision an angry monarch pacing the floor, reenacting the scene he had just witnessed in Blackfriar Hall, increasingly settling on Bishop Fisher as the object of his obsessive wrath. How dare that man? With the first asserted, "No sir, not I," Fisher had articulated his death warrant. Maybe not immediately, but inevitably. For everyone knew the king would get what he wanted. As his henchmen made clear: *indignatio principis mors est*,[24] "the wrath of the king is death." Fisher's execution would indeed occur six years later almost to the day, on June 22, 1535.[25]

Yes, he was "but one man." Even so, the king would not brook any man contesting his authority, even his aggressive assertion of authority over not just the temporal affairs of England but the Church as well. Fisher had to know this, but spoke with strength to power nonetheless. Macklem concludes his narrative, "The effect of Fisher's words must have been breathtaking. And yet they are of a piece with everything we know of the man. No one else in the kingdom would have dared to give the lie in public to the Archbishop of Canterbury and the King." [26]

This stand on conscience begins our exploration of the thoughts, words, and conduct of John Fisher and Thomas More. What each man learned, and what each man teaches, is that there are times when truth is elusive and times when it is not, but in either case, the pursuit of truth requires a costly expenditure of time, study, and prayer. Still more, a conscience fixed upon truth, once obtained, requires action, and that action often costs us dearly. But the price paid plumes to peace thereafter.[27]

Chapter 2

Truth

"For a man may in such case lose his head and have no harm."

"For it was much against my conscience."

That is what John Fisher said in response to the anger of the king directed squarely at him in Blackfriar Hall. The primacy of conscience at the center of Fisher's response is reminiscent of his friend Thomas More. When summoned to Lambeth Palace to take the oath attendant to the Act of Succession, More refused to sign the oath, saying, "My purpose is not to put any fault either in the Act or any man that made it, or in the oath or any man that swears it, nor to condemn the conscience of any other man. But as for myself in good faith my conscience so moves me in the matter, that though I will not deny to swear to the succession, yet unto the oath that here is offered to me, I cannot swear without the jeopardizing of my soul to perpetual damnation."[28]

To More and Fisher, eternal consequences accompanied the taking of an oath. To speak against their conscience consisted of putting their souls at risk. They wanted to go to heaven and knew you couldn't get there on featherbeds, that it entailed suffering, abandonment, and detachment.[29]

The world in their day, and who doubts but ours too, was ordered and arranged around other things—lust, power, comfort, fame—not around the straight and narrow that leads to eternal life.

What is the conscience that both More and Fisher kept coming back to? In one letter from prison, More mentions "conscience" forty times, but what exactly did he mean? Robert Bolt, the twentieth-century author of the incomparable play *A Man For All Seasons*, understood him to mean it as a possession of self. To Bolt, More was a "hero of self-hood" who had "an adamantine sense of his own self."[30]

I see More (and Fisher) differently. They were not self-confident but rather "Christ-confident." They were not adamantine followers of self-will but servants of the one true God who spoke through his Word and his Church. Their strength of conviction was rooted in their shared belief that God was truth and that his Church was a truth-telling institution. And *rooted* is the right word, not free-floating. Vincent of Lerins spoke to this sense of conscience rooted in the law of God when he described faith in the fifth century: *quod ubique, quod semper, quod ab omnibus creditum est*[31]—"what has been believed everywhere, always, by all." More and Fisher shared a notion that one's conscience must be formed by the unchanging dictates of faith, ever ancient, ever new.

The centrality of conscience is not located in the supreme self but rather in submission to eternal truth. Not More's truth or Fisher's truth, or even the king's truth, but ultimate truth. The sixteenth century was a time of turbulence, new ideas, exciting discoveries (the printing press for one), and everything seemed up for grabs. More and Fisher found themselves in the middle of this exciting time as members of a group called the "humanists," who advocated the "new learning." Fisher, for example, brought Erasmus and the study of Greek to Cambridge University. More, for his part, championed the education of women, demanding the same level of academic excellence from his daughters as he did his son. This new learning influenced positive effects in such areas as law, education, public hygiene, and public administration. Some in their group of humanists saw the new learning as an opportunity to jettison the anchors of the past. Fisher and More disagreed. They were change agents rooted in ultimate *verities*.

The new learning led some to question the authority of the Church, "and dared to claim that each man was his own priest."[32] But here Fisher and More parted ways with their fellow humanist reformers. Describing Fisher, Macklem says:

> He was not indifferent to the evils that flourished in the Church. On the contrary, he had raised his voice against them again and again, while over the years the austerity of his life had spoken of his sincerity more eloquently than any words. Moreover, he was among the few who had recognized the importance of learning to a progressive understanding of man and his place in the world. He knew that much remained to be done, but it never occurred to him to question the supreme importance of the Church as the living center of the religious life of the people.[33]

To them, conscience was tethered to truth, the truth of Christ as taught by his holy Church. In this sense, they anticipated the teachings of John Henry Newman three centuries later. In his *Letter to the Duke of Norfolk*,[34] Newman contrasted the English emphasis on the "rights" of conscience, what he calls the "Englishman's prerogative" to be master in all things, to the prevenient "duties" of conscience that so clearly animated the likes of More and Fisher. It is not the right of self-will but the duty to obey the divine voice within. That divine voice—conscience—speaks to issues of right and wrong, reconciliation, justice, truth, wisdom, sanctity benevolence, and mercy. Properly informed, it is sovereign, irreversible, absolute in its authority.[35] As Pope John Paul II would later say during a speech I was fortunate enough to attend many years ago,[36] if we have freedom to choose, we have a duty to choose wisely. Fisher and More recognized their respective duty to properly inform their conscience, to ascertain the divine voice within; but once informed, they understood their duty to act according to it: *fiat justitia ruat caelum.*[37] To do otherwise meant the potential loss of their soul.

Earthly potentates were to be respected and in temporal things obeyed. But they simply held no sway over the conscience, the divine command, of either man. More tells his daughter that if it were possible to please both the king and the king of kings, no one would be more willing to take the oath than him:

> But since standing my conscience I can in no wise do
> it, and that for the instruction of my conscience in the
> matter, I have not slightly looked, but by many years

studied, and advisedly considered, and never could yet
see nor hear that thing, nor I think I never shall, that
could induce mine own mind to think otherwise than
I do, I have no other remedy that God hath given me
. . . that either I must displease Him, or abide any
worldly harm that He shall for mine other sins, under
name of this thing suffer to fall upon me . . . yet if
I had not trusted that God should give me strength
rather to endure all things, than offend my conscience,
you may be very sure I would not have come here.[38]

Informed conscience, subservient to truth, and obedient to
Christ's vicar on earth, lets this "one man," John Fisher, and
this man for all seasons, Thomas More, stand for truth and,
when necessary, against the king. They stand resolutely and
respectfully defiant to a king who demands too much. When
first approached to consider Henry's great matter, Fisher
spent two years "[devoting] himself to a scrupulous study
of the Scriptural authorities and opinions of the Fathers. . . .
He had taken great pains to arrive at the truth and he could
not change his mind without injury to . . . his conscience."[39]
More, likewise "by many years studied, and advisedly considered" the king's "great matter."[40]

In both cases, the men studied, tested their ideas, sought
advice from others, and gathered more information. And
they prayed, and only then did they decide. And once
decided, they were resolute, unwavering, come what may. It
was this confidence in a well-formed conscience that seemed
to others either the epitome of bravery or stupidity.

Remarkably, although conscience reigned supreme in each man's mind and heart, both adamantly refused to judge the conscience of others. Fisher wrote, "Not that I condemn any other men's conscience. Their conscience may save them; and mine must save me." To a friend, More wrote that "each man must decide how to answer the oath in the privacy of his own conscience." In Bolt's play, *A Man for All Seasons,* More responds to a friend's petition that he come with them (in the signing of the oath) for fellowship, "and when you go to heaven for following your conscience and I am consigned to hell for not following mine, will you come with me . . . for fellowship?"[41]

This sense of eternal consequence attendant to the following of conscience is the motivating principle of each man's life, as it was the key to the mental peace they possessed in the midst of turmoil. More's comment to his daughter puts his reliance on God nicely: "I verily trust in God. He shall rather strengthen me to bear the loss, than against this conscience to swear and put my soul in peril."[42] He went on to say, after a series of interrogations, the obvious result of which was, especially to a lawyer as brilliant as More, that the king intended for his execution: "And while it might perhaps seem to be a small cause for comfort because I might take harm here first in the meanwhile, I thanked God that my case was such in this matter through the clearness of my own conscience that though I might have pain I could not have harm, for a man may in such case lose his head and have no harm."[43]

In addition to the sense of eternal consequences that attended any serious violation of conscience, More and

Fisher relied, for their strength, heavily on the communion
of saints and the knowledge that they were being asked to
assent to something that had been denied for a thousand
years. Fisher represented his position as the result of two
years of study of the Scripture and the Fathers. More, the
first and only layman summoned to swear to the oath,
resisted despite being asked to weigh his conscience against
the opposition of all the lords and bishops who had signed
the oath. More responded that he stood with the general
councils of all of Christendom. He understood that England
was an island both in the geographic sense but also in the
sense of the course of Christendom over a thousand years.
In this he was lining up squarely with Augustine, and later
John Henry Newman, who guided their conducts by the
saying "*securus judicat orbis terrarum*" (the secure judgment
of the whole world is right). More and Fisher did not fight
alone. They were surrounded by a great cloud of witnesses.
To his daughter Meg, from his prison cell awaiting execution, More "affirmed the unity of Christendom as well as
the inherited doctrines of those holy doctors and saints who,
rejoicing in the presence of God, sustained the communion
of the faithful upon earth."[44]

More confirmed this in his allocution "in the discharge
of his conscience" after the jury took fifteen minutes to find
him guilty of treason: "This Indictment is grounded upon an
act of parliament directly repugnant to the laws of God and
his Holy Church. . . . This Realm, being but one member
and small part of the Church, might not make a particular
law disagreeable with the general law of Christ's universal
Catholic Church."[45] Upon an accusation of maliciousness,

More repeated, "Nay, nay, very and pure necessity, for the discharge of my conscience, forces me to speak so much. Wherein I call and appeal to God, whose only sight pierces into the very depth of man's heart, to be my witness."[46] What a hero!

Lawyers say that words matter. And they are right. But conduct matters too. And More and Fisher knew that when one acts consistently with a properly formed conscience, one lives free even when consigned to a prison tower; one lives courageously even when the forces of the king are arrayed against you; one dies heroically, even humorously, in the knowledge that the One served is beckoning "well done my good and faithful servant," of the king, and God first.

CHAPTER 3

Oath

"Is not an oath words we say to God?"

As a federal judge (and former federal prosecutor), I have observed more than a thousand witnesses take an oath. I have also had occasion to take an oath and provide testimony myself. It is a remarkable phenomenon, this oath-taking, testimony-giving thing. It never gets old.

A name is called. A citizen enters from the back of the courtroom and walks up the center aisle. Invariably, all eyes are upon her. When she enters the well of the courtroom, she approaches the clerk's table, puts her left hand on the Bible, raises her right hand, and swears "to tell the truth, the whole truth, and nothing but the truth, so help me God." It is a solemn promise that sets the tone for the testimony that follows.

In other contexts, I have taken and administered oaths; for instance, at weddings, oaths of office as a federal employee, judicial oaths, and oaths of loyalty to the Constitution. Each time I am struck by the significance of the words uttered and the commitments involved: to have and to hold from this day forward; to protect and defend the Constitution against all enemies; to administer justice to the rich and to the poor. Sometimes referred to as "sacred oaths," these words, these commitments, undergird the integrity of our society and our very system of justice.

Our statutes continue to convey the seriousness of the oath and the duties incumbent on the oath-taker. For example, in my home state of North Carolina, General Statute Section 11-1 states:

> Oaths and affirmations are to be administered with solemnity:
>
> Whereas, lawful oaths for discovery of truth and establishing right are necessary and highly conducive to the important end of good government; and being most solemn appeals to Almighty God, as the omniscient witness of truth and the just and omnipotent avenger of falsehood . . . such oaths ought to be taken and administered with the utmost solemnity.[47]

The North Carolina statute further requires the party to be sworn to "lay his hand upon the Holy Scriptures, in token of his engagement to speak the truth and in further token that, if he should swerve from the truth, he may be justly deprived of all the blessings of that holy book and may be liable to that vengeance which he has imprecated on his own head."[48]

Of course, exceptions are made for witnesses who may have philosophical or religious scruples with the taking of an oath on the Bible. In these circumstances, however, the oath required shall be administered in the following manner:

He shall stand with his right hand lifted up towards heaven, in token of his solemn appeal to the Supreme God, and also in token that if he should swerve from the truth he would draw down the vengeance of heaven upon his head, and shall introduce the intended oath with these words, namely:

I, A.B., do appeal to God, as a witness of the truth and the avenger of falsehood, as I shall answer the same at the great day of judgment, when the secrets of all hearts shall be known.[49]

The clear sentiments expressed in these North Carolina statutes give a glimpse into the understanding that our two saints must have had in sixteenth-century England. The issue of the taking of the oath is inextricably interwoven with the issue of conscience that formed the core principle of More's and Fisher's reactions to the king's demands.

More's conscience did not permit him to swear to the king's oath. Being a prudential diplomat and public servant, he was content with remaining silent as to Henry's "great matter." He believed that according to the law, silence implied consent, so that at best, the only inference one could legally draw from More's silence was his assent to a given proposition. And he was able for a time by remaining silent to navigate the dangerous waters of the king's insistence on his oath-taking. He said nothing to anyone about the great matter, being "innocent as a dove, wise as a serpent." But Henry's tolerance with More, Fisher, and others who did not come to heel in response to his command came to an end. He demanded submission by the taking of an affirmative oath, to the factual predicates supporting the royal succession through Anne Boleyn, and ultimately to recognize his position as Supreme Head of the Church in England. This fealty the men in question could not give him.

More's stand on conscience is poignantly articulated in a conversation with his beloved daughter Meg, "the person he loved more than anyone else except God."[50] Meg, for her part, adored her father. She could not bear the thought of his imprisonment, much less his execution. In a beautiful exchange from *A Man for All Seasons*, she implores him to take a step back from his "scruple of conscience."

> More: You want me to swear to the Act of
>   Succession?
> Margaret: God more regards the thoughts of the
>   heart than the words of the mouth. Or so you've
>   always told me.
> More: Yes.
> Margaret: Then say the words of the oath and in your
>   heart think otherwise.
> More: What is an oath then but words we say to
>   God?
> Margaret: That's very neat.
> More: Do you mean it isn't true?
> Margaret: No, it's true.
> More: Then it is a poor argument to call it "neat,"
>   Meg. When a man takes an oath, Meg, he's holding
>   his own self in his own hands. Like water. And if
>   he opens his fingers then—he needn't hope to find
>   himself again. Some men aren't capable of this, but
>   I'd be loath to think your father one of them.[51]

Many in the time of More and Fisher accused them of a con-
trivance, a scruple, even a lawyer's trick; after all, everyone
else took the oath, why not you? Kipling insightfully wrote,
"If you can trust yourself when all men doubt you, but make
allowance for their doubting too."[52] Isn't this a classic case of
too much self-trust and too little accommodation?

More's daughter Meg seems to express this incredulity.
With regard to the oath, she urged her father to speak words
but believe otherwise in his heart. In my own career, I have
seen someone take an oath with his fingers crossed. And
I have often suspected that others have testified with that
attitude, just not so blatantly expressed. The casualness of
the oath to some in More's day, to many in our own day, is
troublesome.

More, the former judge and lord chancellor, cherished the
truth producing character of the oath and recoiled from the
eternal consequences attendant to the giving of false testimony under oath. He would recall the oath taken as under
sheriff where he would have sworn "so help me God and all
the saints."[53] That attitude is manifest in More's reaction to
Richard Rich's perjury at More's trial for treason. One of the
counts was based entirely on Rich's testimony concerning
a single conversation between the two which had allegedly
taken place in More's prison cell. Rich had been sent to
More's prison cell to remove his writing materials and books.
He testified More had denied Parliament's authority to make
Henry the supreme head of the Church in England. More
denied making any such statement and went a further step
to commit himself to an oath calling God to be his witness:
"If I were a man, my lords, who did not reverence an oath, I

need not, as is well known, stand here as an accused person in this place, at this time, or in this case. And if this oath of yours, Master Rich, be true, then I pray that I never see God in the face, which I would not say, were, it otherwise, to win the whole world. . . . In good faith, Master Rich, I am sorrier for your perjury than for my own peril."[54]

More's understanding of an oath, the same understanding reflected in our modern statutes, if taken seriously, would revolutionize witness testimony. For example, imagine if testimony were given on the following assumptions:

- there is truth and a truth-loving God;
- an oath constitutes a solemn appeal to that God;
- who is both an omniscient witness of truth and
- an omnipotent avenger of falsehood;
- and finally, a recognition that there is a great judgement day when the secrets of all hearts shall be known.

The potential effect on the quality of justice, the resolution of disputes, the reduction in querulous litigation is staggering. Imagine further the application of these principles to our informal relationships, if our "yes" meant yes and our "no" no.

But it is largely not so in our times. Men have opened their hands and let water through. And it often seems difficult to find one's self. Our courts suffer when witnesses take oaths casually. Prosecutors seldom pursue perjury charges. When structural supports for truth-telling and truth-finding breaks down, a cynicism spreads.

Samuel Johnson, the great English philosopher who would appear on the scene two centuries after Fisher and More, admonishes that mankind needs more often to be reminded than informed; consider this your reminder, dear reader.

Our times reflect the energy, creativity, innovation, and optimism reflected in the sixteenth century. It mirrors also the dark side of that century. We are not unfamiliar with potentates using people to get their way, strident civil discourse, suppressed speech, unnecessary wars that consume limited resources and waste human life, definitional problems which obscure the meaning of marriage.

In such times, we are reminded by the historical example of More and Fisher. There are times when a stand for truth, even in the face of overwhelming opposition and adverse personal consequence, is warranted. Words matter, actions matter, truth matters. In an age of casual relativism, we need our "yes" to be yes and our "no" no. We need to speak truth to power, to our communities, to our neighbor. We need Fisher and More.

CHAPTER 4

Vocation

"For God is as mighty in the stable as in the temple."

On October 13, 2019, John Henry Newman was named a Catholic saint, the first Englishman canonized since the English Reformation martyrs, including More and Fisher. Unsurprisingly, Newman possessed an especial love for Thomas More. In the process of his conversion to the Catholic faith, Newman was reassured of the Church's truth-telling characteristics by reflecting on the fact that the eminent Thomas More, "one of the choice specimens of wisdom and virtue,"[55] was willing to die for it. Naturally, he had a great respect for Fisher as well, including a letter written to Pope Leo XIII petitioning for Fisher's canonization.

Newman understood particularly well the notion of calling that informed the lives of Fisher and More. Writing three centuries after their deaths, Newman captured the essence of a calling: "God has created me to do Him some definite service; He has committed some work to me which He has not committed to another. I have my mission—I may never know it in this life, but I shall be told it in the next. Somehow I am necessary for His purposes, as necessary in my place as an Archangel in his—if, indeed, I fail, He can raise another, as He could make the stones children of Abraham. Yet I have a part in this great work."

Like Newman, More and Fisher understood their part in this great work. Each followed different career paths. Each rose to the pinnacle of success in his profession. At every stage there was a separation from the crowd in terms of distinction. More, of course, became the brilliant lawyer. We might look at his career from an American constitutional perspective and say that he served at the highest levels of each branch of government: the legislative (Parliamentary speaker), judicial (judge), and executive (lord chancellor). Fisher, meanwhile, founded two colleges at Cambridge, was president of another, chancellor of Cambridge University, bishop of Rochester, and ultimately a cardinal of the Catholic Church.

But I would suggest that they are known today not for the quality of their resumes[56] but rather for the quality of their character; men of unflinching courage, true to their convictions, and abandoned to God's providence.

Each of us is called to a mission, some work committed uniquely to us, which we may see in a mirror dimly, or not at all. But God has created us in Newman's word as "a link in a chain, a bond of connection between persons," created for good if we but keep his commandments and serve him in our calling.

More sought to convey this sense of mission to those he counseled. One such person was Richard Rich. In *A Man for All Seasons*, Rich is described by Robert Bolt as follows: "Early thirties. A good body unexercised. A studious, unhappy face lit by the fire of banked-down appetite. He is an academic hounded by self-doubt to be in the world of affairs and longing to be rescued from himself."[57]

To this person, before the perjury and betrayal that would turn Rich into a sixteenth-century Judas, More addressed some early career advice. As Bolt portrays it:

> More: The Dean of St Paul's offers you a post, with a house, a servant and fifty pounds a year.
> Rich: What? What post?
> More: At the new school.
> Rich: (*bitterly disappointed*) A teacher?
> …
> More: Why not be a teacher? You'd be a fine teacher. Perhaps even a great one.
> Rich: And if I was, who would know it?
> More: You, your pupils, your friends, God. Not a bad public that…Oh, and a quiet life.
> Rich: (*laughing*) You say that.
> More: Richard, I was commanded into office; it was inflicted on me…(*Rich regards him*) Can't you believe that?
> Rich: It's hard.
> More: (*grimly*) Be a teacher.

As a father, coach, lawyer, and judge, I have had the opportunity to counsel many would be Richard Riches—young, ambitious, cautiously optimistic, professionals desiring to achieve the perceived success they see in front of them. Often dissatisfied with their present place, they long for the next career advancement, not fully comprehending that life is lived in the moment, that they are—right now—a link in the chain. There is an underlying, unspoken angst, a yearning for what's next. But More cautions against this striving anxiety, "God is as mighty in a stable as he is in a temple."[58]

He knew that excessive ambition corrupts: "Such a pestilent serpent is ambition and desire of vainglory and sovereignty that among those whom he once enters, he creeps forth so far till with division and variance he turns all to mischief: First, longing to be next to the best; afterward, equal with the best; and at last, chief and above the best."[59]

Fisher, likewise, focuses laser-like on the notion of vainglory in his funeral sermon honoring King Henry VII:

> Where are now the kings and princes that once reigned over all the world, whose glory and triumph were lifted up above the earth? . . . Where are they now whom we have known and seen in our days in such great wealth and glory that it was thought by many they would never have died, never have been forgotten? . . . Are they not gone and wasted like smoke? . . . St. James compares the vanity of this life to a vapor, and he says it shall perish and wither away as a flower in the hay season (James 4:15).[60]

More and Fisher's lives seem to stand for something else: for the proposition that the purposeful life is accomplished more by performing well the tasks set before us rather than anxiously anticipating the next thing. More, for example, was a brilliant foreign ambassador, a respected high-sheriff, a compassionate judge known for his honesty, a trusted advisor to the king, and most importantly, an engaged father. He excelled at that which in the moment he was called to do. Fisher performed his duties with such excellence that he was named chancellor of Cambridge for life!

This excellence in action can be juxtaposed to the compromising and conniving approaches of some friends and adversaries. Consider More's and Erasmus's very different reactions to threats of recrimination. The latter said, "Mine was never the spirit to risk my life for the truth. Not everyone has the strength needed for martyrdom. I fear that, if strife were to break out, I shall behave like Peter. When popes and emperors make the right decision I follow, which is godly; if they decide wrongly I tolerate them, which is safe." More responded differently. "My Lords," he said, "these terrors be arguments for children."[61] And on another occasion, "Is that all, my Lord? Then in good faith there is no more difference between your grace and me, but that I shall die today and you tomorrow." More was right. More died confidently in July 1535 while Erasmus died suddenly of dysentery the next year, almost to the week. "He [More] talks with his friends about a future life in such a way as to make you feel that he believes what he says."[62]

An even starker comparison can be made of More to his adversaries. He described Cardinal Wolsey thus: "Vainglorious was he very far above all measure, and that was a great pity, for it did harm, and made him abuse the great gifts that God had given him."[63]

Wolsey would die in disgrace, saying, "If I had served God as diligently as I have done the King, he would not have given me over in my gray hairs."[64] When he fell out of favor with the king, his subordinate, Thomas Cromwell, took his place of influence. As the king's master secretary, he framed government policy and persecuted those who, like More and Fisher, deigned to pursue an independent path. He was a despotic minister of state who gradually achieved nearly absolute power, and like Wolsey before him, became one of the richest men in England.

Yet today he is forgotten.[65] Hilaire Belloc notes, "For a dozen men who could tell you a fair amount about his master, Henry VIII, or about any other of the prominent figures of the time, there is barely one who could give you much more than the name of Thomas Cromwell."[66]

What *is* known is that the architect of the trumped-up treason charges against More and Fisher would himself eventually be detained by the king and condemned to death without trial, this for his role in "bamboozling" the king into his fourth marriage, the second to a woman named Anne (this time . . . Cleves). Begging for his life, he pleaded "mercy, mercy, mercy" to the king, whom he compared to God and proclaimed that the perfume of the royal hand would waft him to heaven if he were but allowed to kiss it once again. Not the kind of expression that prompts emulation. There would be no mercy, no ring-kissing, no remembrances. "Cromwell had served his purpose," notes More biographer Peter Ackroyd, "having enriched the king with the dissolution of the monasteries, and could now be dispatched from the scene."[67]

And finally, what happened to our teacher in waiting turned perjurer Richard Rich? At his trial, after his testimony provided the only evidence against his former mentor, Bolt has More admonishing him. "Why Richard, it profits a man nothing to give his soul for the whole world . . . but for Wales?"[68] He is not heard from again, famous only for the infamy of his position-acquiring, death-causing testimonial perjury.

Christopher Hollis assesses Rich correctly:

> There have been few, if any, of our race more odious than Rich. He was at that date (More's trial) only at the beginning of his villainies. In the previous month, he had visited Fisher in the Tower and held a conversation with him which he promised would be strictly confidential. This conversation he had revealed at Fisher's trial. Afterwards he joined with Cromwell in suppressing the monasteries and greatly enriched himself from their suppression. Then at Cromwell's fall he turned against him and gave evidence against him at his trial. In the subsequent reaction against the reformers Rich put himself at the head of their persecutors and was present at the racking of Anne Askew.[69] Then with Edward VI's accession he went over to the other side and joined Somerset.[70] He also took part in the proceedings against the Catholic bishops. On Edward's death he signed the proclamation of Jane Grey,[71] but seeing her chance of success to be small, declared instead for Mary and on her accession was sworn by her council. He was appointed to the commission to try Northumberland.[72] He returned to Catholicism and, to prove the sincerity of his reconversion showed especial rigour in his persecution of reformers. He survived into Elizabeth's reign but by then was too old for

further tergiversations. It is a comfort both for Catholics and Protestants to reflect that a high proportion
of the acts of persecution of those horrid times were
perpetrated by timeservers and turncoats, themselves
of no faith but ready to slay in order to give a colour of
sincerity to the cat's last turn in the pan.[73]

More and Fisher's eternal perspective inoculated them from
the corruption caused by "the serpent of ambition." Gov-
erned by the sense that I might die today and you tomorrow,
it was not, they believed, the inevitable fact of death that
matters but the purposeful life led up to the point of death
that counts.

In his unfinished *History of King Richard III*,[74] More
alludes to the Greek poet Lucian: "These matters be king's
games, as it were stage plays, and for the most part played
upon scaffolds."[75] The sycophants of today, he knew, would
inexorably face the ax of execution tomorrow. In the tyrannical, totalitarian Tudor age in which he lived, it has been
estimated that up to eighty-five thousand people were executed,[76] the ax falling upon the neck of the just and the unjust
at royal whim. But what a difference. The conscientious man
of faith dies believing his execution is but the gateway to
eternal life. The vain seeker of status dies crying out his last
disillusioned gasp of earthbound agony. Shakespeare could
have been channeling More and Fisher in *Macbeth*, a story of
carnage caused by the corrupting effect of worldly ambition
achieved at any cost. In lamenting Lady Macbeth's suicide,
Macbeth hauntingly echoes More's stage play metaphor:

> She should have died hereafter
> There would have been time for such a word
> Tomorrow, and tomorrow, and tomorrow,
> Creeps in this petty pace from day to day,
> To the last syllable of recorded time;
> And all our yesterdays have lighted fools
> The way to dusty death. Out, out, brief candle!
> Life's but a walking shadow, a poor player,
> That struts and frets his hour upon the stage,
> And then is heard no more. It is a tale
> Told by an idiot, full of sound and fury,
> Signifying nothing.[77]

We should live significant lives, but our significance must be rightly ordered behind the significance of God, for only then can we discern our life's vocation and fulfill it in accord with his will. Don't be a Wolsey or Cromwell working your whole life for the wrong things, a Rich who would do so much for so little, or a king who would die a venereal death. Be a More, be a Fisher. They pursued excellence in striving after God's providential will, nothing more, nothing less, nothing else. Having achieved extraordinary success, they demonstrated a remarkable willingness to let it all go in service to a higher calling. Neither man seemed more at peace than when confined to the Tower. It seems that the source of their peace was beyond their achievements, that their achievements might in fact reflect their set purpose of bringing glory to God.

More demonstrates this point clearly in a conversation he had with his beloved daughter while confined in his prison cell. He tells her the king has taken nothing from him but his liberty. By doing so, Henry has done him "great good by the spiritual profit he has received."[78] He thinks of St. Peter upon the water:

> Mistrust Him, Meg, will I not, though I feel me faint. Yea, and though I should feel my fear even at point to overthrow me too, yet shall I remember how Saint Peter with a blast of wind began to sink for his faint faith, and shall do as he did, call upon Christ and pray Him to help. And then I trust he shall set His holy hand unto me, and in the stormy seas, hold me up from drowning. . . . I shall therefore with good hope commit myself wholly to Him. . . . And therefore, mine own good daughter, never trouble thy mind for anything that ever shall happen to me in this world. Nothing can come but that God will. And I make me very sure that whatsoever that be, seem it never so bad in sight, it shall indeed be the best.[79]

With a sense of calling and submission to God's sovereignty, More can be at peace, even "merry," in the midst of the storm.

In an exploration of the concept of vocation, there is yet another consideration. When More was a youth, he sensed he might have a calling to be a Carthusian monk. For three years while studying the law, he lived on the grounds of the Charterhouse, the Carthusian monastery in London, attempting to discern whether he was called to the monastic life. Eventually, he concluded he was not. He became a lawyer instead, a quite good one, whose wisdom, talent, and industry led him to the king's court.

But by the mysterious hand of Providence, and the vengefulness of the king, the Carthusian monks were also confined at the same time as was Thomas More. Peter Ackroyd would note the vocational irony: "He [More] had in a sense returned to the time of his early adulthood, when he had participated in the rituals and services of the London Charterhouse. He had become a monk at last."[80] One scholar, Bernard Basset, surmised, "It could well be that God led More from the Charterhouse for this only reason, that a King's servant should put God first."[81]

More "the monk" and his friends the Carthusian monks were not alone. More's friend John Fisher also landed in the Tower at the same time. Within weeks of each other they would be executed one by one. The Carthusian monks would be the first to die, and upon seeing them led to their execution through the Tower window, More exclaimed to his daughter, "Lo, does thou not see Meg, that these blessed fathers be now as cheerfully going to their deaths as bridegrooms to their marriage?"

Quite independent of this conversation between father and daughter, John Fisher, the next to die, reaches the same conclusion. On the day of his death, Fisher dressed up in his finest clothes and told his servant that this was his marriage day. When death came to More a few weeks later, he was reunited with the Carthusians, and with Fisher, as he told his executioner: "Friend, be not afraid of your office. You send me to God."[82]

Before moving on, we would do well to point out yet another connection between More and the Carthusians. More's stepdaughter, Margaret Clement, had lent succor to the imprisoned Carthusian monks during their imprisonment. Among other things, she let down food to them through the Tower roof. Oftentimes, she would dress as a milkmaid and gain entrance for the purpose of feeding and washing the imprisoned monks. Thirty-five years to the day after More's martyrdom in 1535, as Margaret lay dying in Belgium, she had a vision: "Calling her husband therefore, she told [him] that the time of her departing was now come, for that there were standing about her bed the reverend monks of the Charterhouse, who she had relieved in prison in England, and did call upon her to come away with them, and that therefore she could no longer stay because they did expect her."[83]

Margaret Clement, raised in More's household, instructed by him in the Faith and in intentional living, was comforted at the moment of death by the very people she ministered to in life.

The faithful step-daughter, the joyful monastics, the observant More, and the irenic Fisher were united in death, geographically, temporally, and spiritually, because each had faithfully lived out their quite different vocations. How different things might have turned out if More had entered the monastery, or if the Carthusians had resisted their callings, or if Fisher had remained silent in Blackfriar Hall? They are a link in a chain, a bond of connection to each other, and to us. They kept his commandments, served him in their

quite different callings. And if they were right, live merrily
together with him forever.

CHAPTER 5

Virus

"What our lot brings us, must be borne."

It is not difficult to see the events and tenor of the sixteenth century as a reflection of our twenty-first-century conduct and thought. The adage that there is nothing new under the sun seems apt when we consider the similarities that exist in the two cultures, despite the five hundred years that separate them.

On the political scene, one notes the fear gripping the Tudor kings about palace coups. Henry himself suspected John Fisher and Thomas More of colluding with the government of Spain to overthrow his administration. The word *collusion* should sound familiar to anyone who has lived through the late 2010s. And we have already seen the similarities between the Supreme Court confirmation hearing of Brett Kavanaugh and the legatine inquiry into the marital conduct of Arthur and Catherine.

But perhaps no starker parallel emerges than the virus that lay silent siege to both our time and the time in which Fisher and More lived.

In the year 1517, as More served as under-sheriff of London and John Fisher served as both bishop of Rochester and chancellor of Cambridge University, London and the surrounding areas were besieged by an outbreak of the "sweating sickness." Believed to be caused by an unknown species of the *Hantavirus*, it was a mysterious and contagious disease that came and went only to surge again. Its symptoms included myalgia, headache, abdominal pain, vomiting, and delirium, which were followed by cardiac palpitation, paralysis, and finally, death. The onset of symptoms was sudden, with death often occurring in hours. Thousands lost their lives throughout the numerous iterations of the disease over a sixty-six year period (1485–1551). Those who could afford to left the city; those who stayed had to notify authorities when the virus struck a family member. They were subject to strict quarantine measures, with whole households being shut-up.[84]

In conjunction with the calamity caused by the *Hantavirus*, an immigration dispute led to an outbreak of rioting in the streets of London known as Evil (or Ill) May Day. These violent eruptions stemmed from the pent-up anger of townspeople over the privileges enjoyed by certain foreign merchants, the Lombards. The Lombards were heavily engaged in money-lending, banking. They were commercial merchants who established themselves on "Lombard street." They were resented for making money on the backs of Englishmen and remitting profits to Italy and hated for their perceived arrogance and insolence, as well as their ability to hide behind ambassadorial privilege for protection.

The resentment was articulated in art form in an unpub-
lished Elizabethan play:

> To you all the worshipful lords and masters of this
> city that will take compassion over the poor people
> your neighbors, and also of the great importable hurts,
> losses, and hindrances whereof proceedeth extreme
> poverty to all the King's subjects that inhabit within
> this city and suburbs of the same. For so it is that
> aliens and strangers eat the bread from the fatherless
> children, and take the living from all the artificers, and
> the intercourse from all merchants, whereby poverty
> is so much increased that every man bewaileth the
> misery of other, for craftsmen be brought to beggary,
> and merchants to neediness. Wherefore, the premises
> considered, the redress must be of the commons knit
> and united to one part. And as the hurt and damage
> grieveth all men, so must all men set to their willing
> power for remedy, and not suffer the said aliens in
> their wealth, and the natural born men of this region
> to come to confusion.[85]

A match was lit when one particular foreign merchant
sexually propositioned a Londoner's wife and boasted that
if the woman had been the mayor's wife, "had I once in my
possession, I would keep her in spite of him that does say
nay."[86] The propositioned woman provocatively responded,
"I am ashamed that freeborn Englishmen, having beaten
foreigners within their own bounds, should thus be braved
and abused by them at home."[87]
   It was on.

Agitators organized demonstrations against the Lombards. Householders were warned to stay indoors or face injury. Curfews were imposed and violated. Communications about the shut-down were muddled. People ignored orders to dispel and pelted the streets with clubs and bricks and shouts of violence. The chaotic scene was described by a contemporary in these words:

> Then out at every door came clubs and weapons. . . .
> Then more watermen. . . . There . . . met with them Sir
> Thomas More and others, desiring them to go to their
> lodgings. And as there were entreating, and had almost
> brought them to a stay, the people of St Martin's threw
> out stones and bats (bricks), and hurt diverse honest
> persons that were persuading the riotous people to
> cease, and they bade them hold their hands, but still
> they threw out bricks and hot water. Then a sergeant-
> at-arms called Nicolas Downe, which was there with
> Master More, entreating them, being sore hurt, in a
> frenzy cried "Down with them!" Then all the misruled
> persons ran to the doors and windows of St. Martin's
> and spoiled all they found and cast it into the street.[88]

King Henry VIII and Lord Chancellor Wolsey were furious. Hundreds of people were arrested, so many that some had to be housed in churches. Felonious conduct could be sanctioned by death, and thirteen rioters went to the gallows. It could well have been more but for the efforts of the under-sheriff More. After attempting his best to quell the riot, More approached the crown on behalf of the city requesting a pardon for the rioters. The result of his efforts was that hundreds subject to execution were pardoned, despite Wolsey's objections.

More's mediating efforts were celebrated in an Elizabethan play, *The Booke of Sir Thomas More*. It was never performed because of the censor's objection to the representation of an anti-alien riot on stage. But the manuscript survives and the spirit of it shines in these lines:

> Sir Thomas More humbly upon his knee
> Did beg the lives of all, since on his word
> They did so greatly yield. The king hath granted it,
> And made him Lord High Chancellor of England.

After receiving the king's pardon, the propositioned woman who herself faced the gallows for her role in the quashed insurrection declares:

> More's name may live for this right noble part.
> And whenso'er we talk of Ill May Day,
> Praise More.[89]

The effective law enforcement action by More followed by his compassionate appeals on behalf of those arrested is of a kind with his character. He saw the big picture, and while working effectively to establish order, he did not forget that the people he dealt with were made in the image of God and deserved his respect and his compassion. Largely ignored by historians, his reaction to riotous behavior foreshadows his later course of dealing with adversity.

And what of the *Hantavirus* and concomitant "sweating sickness?" Sadly, the More family and Fisher's diocese would encounter it again and again. It is believed that King Henry

VIII's brother Arthur succumbed to it in 1502. One won-
ders how history might have been altered if Arthur had not
died at an early age, or if he and Catherine had conceived
a male heir. But beyond that speculation, the *Hantavirus*
wreaked other havoc. It surged again and again between the
years 1485 and the final outbreak in 1551. Described as a
"recurrent menace in Tudor Times,"[90] we see it particularly
in 1506, 1507, 1517–18, and 1528. Thousands died at a
time. More's first wife, Joanna, probably succumbed to this
disease (although some attribute her early death at age twen-
ty-nine to influenza). In the spring of 1528, More's daughter Margaret fell into a *Hantavirus* induced coma which led
her doctors to give up all hope of her recovery. But More
had trained for moments like this when the forces of evil or
illness seemed overwhelming: "Whereupon going up after
his usual manner, into his aforesaid New Building, there in
his chapel, on his knees, with tears most devoutly besought
Almighty God that it would like his goodness, unto whom
nothing was impossible, if it was his blessed will, at his mediation to vouchsafe graciously to hear his humble petition."[91]

This description of going to prayer in his "secret oratory"
manifests years of theological study and learned dependence
on God. It is worth analyzing step-by-step to learn the secret
of More's tenacity in confronting adversity:

  -Going up
  -after his usual manner
  -in his chapel, on his knees
  -with tears
  -most devoutly besought

-Almighty God
-that it would like his goodness
-unto whom nothing is impossible
-if it was his blessed will
-at his mediation
-vouchsafe graciously to hear his humble petition.

His petition was granted. While on his knees, More remembered a possible remedy that had not yet been tried called a "clyster," similar to an enema. More left the chapel, consulted the physicians, and begged them to apply the remedy. The doctors admitted they had not thought of it before but willingly applied it. Margaret soon awoke to the joy of a grateful family.

Others were less fortunate. Later, More writes Erasmus about the plague and the death of a friend:

> We are in greater distress and danger than ever; deaths are frequent all around us, almost everybody at Oxford, Cambridge and here in London, having been laid up during the last few days, and very many of our best and most honored friends being lost. Among these—I am distressed to think how it will distress you—has been our friend Andrew Ammonio, in whom both good letters and all good men have suffered a grievous loss. He thought himself protected against contagion by his temperate habits and attributed it to this that, whereas he scarcely met any person whose family had not been sick, the malady had not attacked any one of his. This boast he made to me and others not many hours before his death. For in sweating sickness, as

they call it, no one dies but on the first day. I with
my wife and children am as yet untouched; the rest of
my family recovered. I can assure you that there is less
danger upon a field of battle than in this town.[92]

More's reaction to the virus's devastation is consistent with
his later response to his own misfortune. He concludes his
letter to Erasmus with this assessment: "But what is one to
do? What our lot brings us must be borne, and I have composed my mind for every event."

Prayer, resignation to God's will, and insistence that all
things that come to us are filtered through the hand of a loving God. These habitual responses were formed in the mind
of More early on and sustained him for a lifetime.

Shortly after Meg's bout with the sweating sickness, an
absent More received word that a disastrous fire had destroyed
parts of his home at Chelsea and all of his barns. He would
not panic. Instead, he writes to his family and advises them
to be "merry." He tells everyone to go to Church and give
thanks. He sees in the fire an act of divine providence whose
purport is to teach him and his family the insignificance of
material things. His only lingering concern is for the neigh-
bors' losses and vows to make them whole, even though the
fire occurred at a difficult financial time for the Mores.

And here is found the mystical key to More's unrelent-
ing optimism, his determination to be thankful, and to be
"merry." Like Job, More's later years, after a lifetime of bless-
ing from God, are beset by adversity. He walks away from
a penultimate position as lord chancellor of England. He
endures a growing sense of penury, which will only get worse

with time as he increasingly becomes the target of Henry's wrath, rendering him essentially unemployable. He is arrested, confined in a Tower with limited visitation rights. And when he appears to his tormentors too happily engaged in writing about the passion of Christ, they take his writing utensils away. Improvising, he then writes with coal. Alone, abandoned, imprisoned, approaching execution, in a letter to his kindred spirit daughter Meg, More sums up his philosophy of life: "Therefore, my own good daughter, never trouble your mind over anything that ever shall happen to me in this world. Nothing can come but what God wills. And I make myself very sure that whatsoever that be, even if it seems ever so bad at sight, it shall indeed be the best. . . . Serve God and be merry and rejoice in him."[93]

More intuits that God works all things for good. *Omnia in bonum.* If God does not deliver him from the lion's den, then he will "in his great mercy" give him the grace and strength to endure their ferocity. Either way, *ad majorem Dei gloriam* (to the greater glory of God).

And so he is merry, exasperatingly so, it seems to one so often encumbered by earthly worries and concerns.

To his apprehensive family, whom he has just told they will descend the stairs of poverty and, if necessary, go begging together singing *Salve Regina,* he says, "and so keep company and be merry together."[94]

To the guard who comes to the tower privately to tell him that he will be executed at 9:00 a.m., who warns him that at his execution the king demands he "not use many words," More responds, "Quit yourself good Pope . . . for I trust that we shall, once in heaven, see each other full and merrily where we shall be sure to live and love together in joyful bliss eternally."[95]

To the judges who condemn him, having already spoken as a Christian lawyer, it was now time to speak simply as a Christian, More says:

> More I have not to say, my lords, but that like as the blessed Apostle St. Paul, as we read in the Acts of the Apostles, was present and consented to the death of St. Stephen and kept their clothes that stoned him to death, and yet they be now both twain holy Saints in heaven and shall continue there friends together forever; so I verily trust and shall right heartily pray that, though your lordships have now here in earth been judges to my condemnation, we may yet hereafter in heaven all merrily meet together to everlasting salvation.[96]

To the weeping guard who escorts him back to the Tower after the death sentence has been pronounced, More says, "Good Master Kingston, trouble not yourself, but be of good cheer, for I will pray for you and my good Lady your wife that we may meet in heaven together where we shall be merry for ever and ever."[97]

And so we return to the foreshadowing event of the *Hantavirus* and bridge it over to More's last days, and his responses to each. More scholar Dr. Gerard Wegemer gets it just right, as he so often does, in assessing More's resolute and peaceful demeanor in the midst of adversity: "Yet he was merry to the end. Why? Because his good humor was not simply a matter of temperament; it was deeply theological, rooted in the cultivated virtues of a faith lived in the present moment, a hope that did not depend on appearances, and a charity rooted in eternity."[98]

More's magnificent, magnanimous legacy merrily beckons today.

Chapter 6

Family

*"I wouldn't change this poor old wife for
the richest widow in England."*

A previous chapter examined the many career achievements of Fisher and More but showed that they are
remembered more for their extraordinary courage, integrity,
and faithfulness. Our current chapter dwells on another
aspect of their character: devotion to family.

At an early age, John Fisher was ordained a priest, and
hence his "marriage to Christ" manifests a different sense of
family. As a parish priest, and later bishop, his family constituted the parishioners for whose eternal souls Bishop Fisher
felt responsible. In an age when absentee bishops were often
the norm, and some like Cardinal Wolsey profited from mul-
tiple benefices (and concomitant income), Bishop Fisher was
ever present in his diocese. It is estimated that he spent 90
percent of his time there, notwithstanding his other duties
as chaplain to the king's mother, college founder, university
chancellor, member of Convocation, and preacher. Despite
all these duties, his heart always turned home—toward his
see.

Fisher was named by Henry VII to the see of Rochester, which was "not a rich prize."[99] It was of little repute, being the smallest, and one of the poorest, dioceses in England. In nominating Fisher, the king admitted having previously promoted less qualified bishops "unadvisedly," but with Fisher, he was promoting someone of "great and singular virtue" in the hope that he would set an example of excellence for other priests. Fisher replaced a bishop who possessed higher ambitions and who, after serving as bishop of Rochester, became bishop of Chichester and then London. It was expected that Fisher would mount the same ladder of ambition, being marked early as a man of talent. But ten years later when he was offered a richer more prestigious see (the see of Lincoln), he refused, saying he "wouldn't change his poor old wife for the richest widow in England."[100] "He regarded Rochester, not merely as a token of royal favor, to be exchanged for a better one at the first opportunity, but as a means of putting to use the long years of study and preparation that were now behind him."[101]

His love for the people he shepherded knew no bounds. He frequently traveled by horseback through his diocese sharing meals of gruel in the smoke-filled huts of his parishioners, performing the role of "alter Christus." He rode through the territory, visiting homes, preaching, and encouraging priests to reform their lives. He did not even spare his fellow bishops, once addressing them in Convocation this way:

> Why should we . . . exhort our flocks to eschew and
> shun worldly ambition, when we ourselves that be
> bishops do wholely set our minds to the same things

we forbid in them? Who can willingly suffer and bear with us in whom preaching humility, sobriety and contempt of the world, they may evidently perceive haughtiness in mind, pride in gesture, sumptuousness in apparel, and damnable excess in all worldly delicates? Truly most reverent fathers, what this vanity in temporal things worketh in you I know not but sure I am that in my self I perceive a great impediment to devotion.[102]

The brilliant preacher and academic scholar was never more at home than when ministering to the needs of his family, the souls he shepherded. Father Vincent McNabb, OP, in his biography *St. John Fisher*, describes well how the bishop attended to his pastoral duties: "Consult your merchants who have travelled many lands; consult your ambassadors and let them tell you whether they have anywhere heard of any bishop who has such love for his flock as never to leave the care of it, even feeding it by word and example, against whose life not even a rash word could be spoken; one who was conspicuous not only for holiness and learning but for love of country."[103]

But Fisher's biological family mattered too. Born in Beverly, England, he was one of four siblings in a religious home. His father died when he was eight years old and his mother remarried, adding four step-siblings to the mix. Fisher was devoted to them all, and they to him. Decades later, when Fisher fell afoul of King Henry VIII and was committed to the Tower, it was his brother Robert who stood by his side. Bishop Fisher was already at an advanced age and in ill health; fifteen long months in a damp cell made things worse. He had a dietary condition that made eating the Tower food barely tenable. Emaciated and going blind, a visitor described him to Cromwell by saying his "body can not bear the clothes on his back."[104]

Without funds of his own, he was reliant on others, chiefly Robert, to provide basic essentials. His brother made sure his diet was as good as it could possibly be under the circumstances and visited him as often as possible. A member of Parliament, Robert was the first to inform Fisher of the recently passed Act of Treason which would eventually result in his death. In an era when prisoners had to pay for their keep, a broken, poor man like Fisher depended on the kindness of his brother and others (in fact he depended too on King Henry, who paid for his doctor visits just to keep him alive long enough to get him to trial).

But few would visit him. To be known as a friend of Fisher invited interrogation, midnight raids, and other investigative efforts. The king effectively isolated Fisher from most human contact. None of that deterred Robert, Fisher's constant friend. He visited frequently, sometimes in disguise, to make sure his condemned brother had human contact. Deprived of most everything, Fisher was not deprived of a brother's love.

And Fisher would give in the same manner that he received. Like More, Fisher used his Tower confinement to write on spiritual subjects. Concerned about his step-sister Elizabeth's religious vocation, he wrote two spiritual meditations for her. Elizabeth, described by her contemporaries as the mirror image of the bishop of Rochester, had entered a Dominican convent. To her, Fisher wrote, "Sister Elizabeth, nothing doth more help effectually to get a good and a virtuous life than if a soul when it is dull and unlusty without devotion, neither disposed to prayer, nor to any other good work, may be stirred or quickened again by fruitful meditation."[105]

How much it must have meant to Elizabeth that her imprisoned brother, contemplating sure execution, took time to compose meditations for the purpose of drawing her soul closer to God.

The second meditation drafted by Fisher for the benefit of his sister, *The Way to Perfect Religion,* demonstrates his ability to step away from academic or theological controversy and provide instruction in everyday spiritual devotion. In it, Fisher analogizes the Christian's pursuit of holiness to the life of a hunter in the field. While some may question the triviality of the comparison, Bishop Fisher knew what he was doing. Much like the Gospel parables, Fisher was able to address spiritual growth in simple but impactful terms. With apologies to the hunter-readers among us, the hunter analogy used by Fisher will be converted to a modern obsession, golf, for greater effect here. Fisher wrote (as modified by this amateur golfer):

> What life is more painful and laborious of itself than is
> the life of the golfer which most early in the morning
> break their sleep and rise when others do take their rest
> and ease, and in his labor he may use no plain path but
> must walk up and down hills, and run over the hedges,
> bushes and streams in search of errant balls and when

necessary cry all the long day "fore", and so continue
without meat or drink until the very night drive him
home. These labors be unto him pleasant and joyous,
for the desire and love that he has for the game of golf.
Verily, verily, if he were compelled to take upon him
such labors, and not for this cause (of golf), he would
soon weary of them, thinking them full tedious unto
him. Neither would he rise out of his bed so soon, nor
fast so long, nor endure these other labors unless he
had a very love therein. For the earnest desire of his
mind is so fixed upon his game, that all these pains
be thought to him but very pleasure. And therefore, I
may well say that *love* is the principal thing that makes
any work easy, though the work be right painful of
itself and that *without love* no labor can be comfortable
to the doer. The love of his game delights him so much
that he cares not for worldly honor. . . . Also the goods
of the world he seeks not for, nor studies how to attain
them. For the love and desire of his game so greatly
occupies his mind and heart. . . . All his mind, all his
soul is busied to know where the next birdie may be
found.[106]

This lengthy (modified) metaphor leads Fisher to the central
point of his meditation for his sister:

Surely if religious persons had so earnest a mind and
desire to the service of Christ, as these golfers to see a
birdie putt, their life should be unto them a very joy
and pleasure. . . . And would to God that in other
things, that is to say, touching worldly honors, worldly

riches, worldly pleasures, would to God that the religious person many of them might profit as much in mindfulness in seeking Christ as the golfer does in seeking his game. And if there were in religious persons as great fervor and love to the service of God as be in golfers to their game all their life should be a very paradise and heavenly joy in this world. And contrariwise without this fervor of love it can not be but painful, weary and tedious to them.

Through a sports analogy, Fisher guides his sister to a more devout life. Perhaps for us who live in a sports saturated culture, it may also have a positive effect: sports, properly directed, can point us to a better way of life, and drawing lessons from the life of sport, we may apply them to the life of the Spirit transforming us here and hereafter.

Extending the sports metaphor in a pivot to Thomas More, his approach to family and fatherhood brings to mind the legendary Chicago Bears halfback Gale Sayers, who recently passed away.[107] Growing up in Chicago, I was mesmerized by Sayers.[108] He was poetry in motion on the football field. Even on slow motion replays, he was a blur, like a ghost gliding across a field. When Sayers retired after a career-ending knee injury, he was replaced in the minds of some Chicago Bear fans by Walter Payton. Although Payton was a legend in his own right, I have never seen anyone who can compare to Sayers.

Readers might wonder what a former Chicagoan-turned-Southerner reminiscing about Gale Sayers could possibly have to do with the sixteenth-century figures under consideration here. It is this. When it came time to write his memoir, Sayers titled it *I Am Third*. By this he meant that God was first, his family second, and he third. This accurately reflects Thomas More's hierarchy of values—more than anything else, he was a family man and an intentional father.

More was a man of the world who succeeded at everything he did. And because of this, he was in high demand. The king wanted his counsel on domestic matters. He wanted him to travel overseas to settle commercial disputes. And he often accompanied Henry and sometimes Wolsey on international diplomacy efforts. He was so proficient a judge in managing his docket that he was called upon more and more to mediate disputes. Wolsey delegated a "mountain of legal cases" to him. In addition to these many duties, he authored many books, including the well-known *Utopia*, while he was in Antwerp on a commercial mission. Writing a book while maintaining a full-time day job is not easy. But More seemed to excel effortlessly. There simply was no flaw in his game.

Yet nothing mattered more than his family. Thomas and Joanna More had four children. When he remarried after her untimely death, he became a father to his wife Alice's daughter. Along the way, he adopted Alice's nurse's daughter after her nurse died. Later, presiding over a case involving horrific childhood abuse, he was granted foster parenting rights to the victim who would eventually become his daughter-in-law. And King Henry himself granted More the wardship of the eldest son of a knight of the realm. Other nephews and nieces and eventually grandchildren would be added to the bustling household.

More insisted that his children and others under his charge develop a disciplined interior life. Morning prayer at his house consisted of the seven penitential psalms,[109] followed by the litanies of the saints. Evening prayers were Psalms 24, 61, and 50 followed by the hymn *Salve Regina* and the *De profundis*.[110] At meals, one of the children read a passage from Scripture followed by comments on what they had read.[111]

More, a firm believer in rigorous education and ahead of his times, established a home school "academy" for his charges. This included girls as well as boys. He was considered a "pioneer in the education of women."[112] He insisted that his daughters be educated to the same extent as his son. Influenced by Plato's contention in the *Republic* that women ought to be as well educated as men, he said, "They are quite capable of it, and their natures are closely related to those of the men."[113] Three of his daughters once engaged in philosophical "disputations" before the king at his palace. One tutor present remarked on the wonder of it and the children's remarkable eloquence. His daughter Margaret, his favorite student, was so brilliant in Greek that she edited the works of Erasmus, the preeminent scholar of Greek literature of his day. Not only would she find errors in his translations but she also discovered on at least one occasion an error in his sourcing as well.[114] Erasmus acknowledged her to be one of Europe's leading female intellectuals, and she would go on to publish a book of her own,[115] a thing unheard of in chauvinistic London.

When because of his duties More was unable to lead the academy, he hired world-class tutors. He laid down expectations of excellence and gave specific instructions in the classical subjects to be covered, including Latin and Greek, the study of the Bible and the early Church Fathers, as well as the new developments in sciences, such as astronomy. When business summoned him away, sometimes months at a time, he required each child to write a daily letter summarizing their activities. His reaction to this daily correspondence is captured in one of his return letters: "I cannot adequately express, my delightful daughters, how greatly pleased I am by your charming letters and no less by the fact, as I notice . . . you yet abandon none of your habits either of dialectic exercises on writing 'themes' or composing verse. This fully convinces me that you love me as you ought, since I observe you feel so much concern in my absence that you practice zealously what you know gives me pleasure when I am with you."[116]

In a letter to their tutor, More insists that in each subject taught, he should "esteem most whatever may teach them piety towards God, charity to all, and modesty and Christian humility in themselves."[117] Only by achieving these "real and genuine fruits of learning" would his children come to possess "solid joy."[118] In his approach, More preferred to "teach virtue rather than to reprove vice and make them love good advice instead of hating it."[119] This emphasis on encouragement fostered in his children a desire to please him rather than to fear him, to please God rather than seek the approval of men, and to pursue excellence to the glory of God rather than be "stirred by praise of flatterers."[120]

More also taught his family the art of letter writing. It was a primary mode of communication between them during his lengthy absences on the king's business. This practice of family letter writing, forged in the crucible of intentional parenting under the pressures of business travel, would have a profound effect after More's incarceration. He was able to smuggle out letters to his daughter Margaret in which he expressed love, communicated guidance and encouragement to his family, and left for posterity "an inflammatory political testament brilliantly camouflaged as an innocuous family letter."[121] This series of letters would form his apologia for his conscience driven actions to a larger audience across the continent and down through time: "They [More and his daughter Margaret] had both realized how the classical art of 'letter' writing as so brilliantly rediscovered by Erasmus could be turned to their advantage. For besides being a mutual conversation between absent friends and a unique and cherished way of reuniting friends and family members whom fate had parted, 'letters' enable their writers to reach out to generations that are yet to be born."[122]

Intuitively adopting a practice he had once put in place long ago, he wrote Margaret knowing she would share his thoughts with others in the family and elsewhere. "And thus have I mine own good daughter disclosed unto you the very secret bottom of my mind." And she would respond: "Mine own entirely beloved father . . ."[123] The intimacy and profundity of this correspondence is worthy of a book. A lifetime of wisdom is contained therein, a few of which are mentioned here:

- In a series of letters, More revealed his deepest thoughts and fears. He did not court martyrdom, he told Meg, but embraced it when necessary: "I have not been a man of such holy living as I might be bold to offer myself to death, lest God for my presumption might suffer me to fall, and therefore I put not myself forward but draw back."[124]

• In a long letter co-written by More and Meg to his step-daughter, Alice Alington, important issues of temptation, reliance on others, and conscience were addressed. The term *conscience* was used over forty times in this one letter alone. More says: "If it were possible for me to do the thing that might content the King's Grace and God therewith not offended, there hath no man taken this oath already more gladly than I." But More's conscience would not let him "do the thing." "But as concerning mine own conscience in this matter (I damn none other man's) is such as may well stand with mine own salvation, therefore am I . . . so sure as that is, God is in heaven."[125] More reveals his heart in these letters and concludes with his signature salutation: "We may meet together in heaven where we shall make merry for ever, and never have trouble after."[126]

More and Meg's correspondence is quoted at length to show the wisdom and love characteristic of More's relationships within his family. Simultaneously, he is mentoring them, strengthening them for the end, giving hope, and leaving a legacy for generations to come.

In addition to the art of letters, More instilled in his children the necessity of a prayer life. One touching demonstration of the habit of prayer instilled in his children occurred during his long incarceration in the Tower. More and Meg frequently prayed the seven penitential psalms together on their knees on the hard floor of his Tower cell. She went a step farther and composed a prayer that she and her father could pray at the same time each day when they were apart. The prayer she composed would penetrate the walls of the Tower and bring comfort and focus to each:

> O Lord, give us grace of your tender pity so firmly to rest our love in you with little regard of this world, and so flee sin and to embrace virtue, that we may say with St. Paul, "To me, to live is Christ and to die is gain," and again "I wish to be discharged and to be with Christ." Send me O Lord, the grace, wretch that I am far, far, farthest of all other from such point of perfection, to amend my life, and continually to have an eye to mine end, without grudge of death, which to them that die in God is the gate of a wealthy life to which God of his infinite mercy bring us all, Amen.[127]

She got it! One can imagine More's heart beaming with the love and even pride of a father. His daughter had listened and learned and become so steeped in her faith that she became a consolation to him in his deepest agony. No longer was he alone, but in prayerful communication with his beloved daughter and the God they mutually loved. Peter Ackroyd describes it this way: "Nothing Meg had ever done in her life had pleased him more. He could see at once from her prayer that she'd fully grasped the point, that it wasn't just the oath, or any single idea, principle or doctrine that had made him defy the tyrannical Henry, but his belief in a redeeming Christ. More (as he and Margaret saw it) could willingly accept death under an unjust law because he had his Savior's example before him."[128]

With Simeon, More could say, "Let your servant go in peace, for my eyes have seen your salvation which you have prepared in the sight of all the nations."[129]

More and his daughter Meg formed the ultimate father-daughter bond without in any way limiting the love More possessed and demonstrated for his wife and other children. Such individual engagement with each child constitutes one of the more significant legacies he left the ages—that of intentional parenting. Every hour More spent raising and forming his children came back to him one hundred fold at the end of his life. This is nowhere more reflected than in the last meeting between him and Meg after his trial.

Meg could not bear to attend the trial, or More would not let her—it is difficult to discern which. But after More's sentence of death was pronounced, he was taken from Westminister Hall to the Tower by a coterie of guards. Led by an ax turned toward More, the now condemned man (for such was the custom), he was escorted along the river toward the Tower. Approaching a narrow drawbridge, he caught sight of Meg, who had waited hours for a glimpse of her father. Returning his gaze, she rushed toward him, forcing her way through the guards. Oblivious to everyone, she flung herself upon her father and kissed him repeatedly. Her conduct is reminiscent of the Magdalen of the Gospels, unsparing, lavishing her affection on the Lord. Here, Meg's kind father looked lovingly but firmly at her and said, "Do not torment yourself. This is God's will."[130]

This gut-wrenching display of affection seemingly had no effect on the guards as they ordered Meg back. They continued the long march over the drawbridge, but suddenly, she ran back to kiss him again for the last time. "Holding her tight and fighting back tears, he begged her to pray to God for the salvation of his soul. Then his face impassive, he released her and walked into the fortress. He did not look back."[131]

But he was not unaffected. In the last letter he ever wrote, he leaves a message for each member of the family. To Meg, he hearkens back to this scene: "I never liked your manner toward me better than when you kissed me last: for I love when daughterly love and dear charity hath no leisure to look to worldly courtesy."[132]

What a poignant scene. The man who rose to the pinnacle of the realm and then yielded everything for truth's sake; the father who cared more for his family than for any worldly gain, and received from his family the love that would help sustain him, now walks alone. Now abandoned to his fate, he takes leave of his beloved Meg. But in doing so, he has provided the intellectual, emotional, and spiritual foundation for his family to survive without him. They have been loved, have known they were loved, and could go on in the certain knowledge that their dad had died their good father, and God's son first.

Chapter 7

Friendship

"He seems to be born and made for friendship."

From an early age, my father counseled me that if you were fortunate, you could count on one hand the number of true friends you possessed. Later, a wise friend told me that if someone says so-and-so is a good guy, one has to ask what he means. Does he mean he is fun to have a beer with? Or is he saying he would trust him to manage his children's trust account? It depends on what the word *good* means.

My father and friend, wittingly or not, are really debating the qualitative aspects of friendship in the Aristotelian sense. In his *Nicomachean Ethics*, Aristotle concludes that *philia*, or "friendship"—meaning people bearing goodwill toward each other—is an essential component of "the good life." He understood there to be three types of friendship. The first he called utilitarian, or friendship based upon mutual benefit. The second is friendship based upon pleasure or delight. Each of these types of friendship add value to life and may even be considered necessary. The third type, however, virtuous friendship, meaning friendship based upon the good of the other, is the worthiest. Being selfless, it bears none of the temporality of the first two. It is enduring. Aristotle considered it the highest form of friendship.

Thomas More exhibited the capacity for virtuous friendship as understood by Aristotle. It is captured charmingly by his friend Erasmus in a letter written to Ulrich von Hutton in 1519. Von Hutton had expressed curiosity about the character of More. In response, Erasmus explained at length that his friend "was born and made for friendship."

> He [More] seems to be born and made for friendship, of which he is the sincerest and most persistent devotee. . . . Accessible to every tender of intimacy, he is by no means fastidious in choosing his acquaintance, while he is most accommodating in keeping it on foot, and constant in retaining it. If he has fallen in with anyone whose faults he cannot cure, he finds some opportunity of parting with him, untying the knot of intimacy without tearing it; but when he has found any sincere friends, whose characters are suited to his own, he is so delighted with their society and conversation, that he seems to find in these the chief pleasure of life. . . . No one takes more pains in attending to the concerns of his friends. What more need I say? If anyone requires a perfect example of true friendship, it is in More that he will best find it. In company his extraordinary kindness and sweetness of temper are such as to cheer the dullest spirit, and alleviate the annoyance of the most trying circumstances.[133]

Centuries after the matters relating to this book, the French would coin a phrase—*fin de siècle*—which in English would roughly translate "turn of the century." In the French usage, it largely, but not exclusively, refers to the end of the century—namely, the nineteenth century. The spirit of *fin de siècle* is often that of ennui, pessimism, and cynicism, but it also hints at the hopefulness of a new century to come.

More's group of friends at the beginning of the sixteenth century was characterized by the hopeful spirit of *fin de siècle*. It was a new age, a new century, and they were engaged in promoting the "new learning" with the zeal and enthusiasm of converts. Other than Erasmus and More, their names are not familiar today: John Colet, William Grocyn, Thomas Linnacre, William Lily, and later, John Fisher. But they were giants of their day, "pioneers of the renaissance in England."[134] Many of them traveled the continent, including Italy, and brought a renewed commitment to classical studies to the English Isle. Colet would preach at, and later become dean of, St. Paul's, founding its famous school. He was Erasmus's intellectual leader and the younger More's spiritual director. Grocyn, for his part, was a lecturer on Greek language and literature at Oxford, and Fisher brought Erasmus to Cambridge to do the same. Erasmus, as noted previously, would become the greatest Greek literature scholar of his day and be known as the figure who "diverted the current of ancient learning from profane to Christian channels."[135]

They were accomplished men in the process of becoming the intellectual leaders of their day. London was the center of the new intellectual life, and through their efforts, the new learning would extend to the universities at Oxford and Cambridge. It was an enthusiastic group of friends fellowshipping at an exciting time. They met together, studied

Greek, read the Fathers, listened to each other's sermons, critiqued each other's writings, and defended one another against the challenges that came their way. One scholar, Frederick Seebohm, referred to them as possessing "a style of human friendship not paralleled outside the Gospel text."[136] They discovered in their pursuit of classical Greek literature maxims that described their friendship: "between friends all is common" and "friendship is equality."[137]

The mutuality of this virtuous friendship can be seen by the influence for good each had on the other. Campbell describes Colet's effect on More: "Counted in the heavenly calculus, it may be, that after his return from Italy, Colet's most important achievement was his influence upon the youthful More then about twenty, Colet's age being thirty-one. Whether it was at Oxford or later that the two first met, it was not long before Colet, a man not given to exaggeration, could pronounce More, as we are told by Erasmus, to be the one genius he had found among his English friends."[138]

And it was obvious that the affection and respect was mutual. Writing to Colet in 1504, More says:

> When I learned not only that you had not returned, but were not to return for a considerable time, I was dejected. What can be more distressing to me than to be deprived of your most dear society, after being guided by your wise counsels, cheered by your charming familiarity, assured by your earnest sermons, and helped forward by your example, so that I used to obey your very look and nod? With these helps I felt myself

strengthened, but without them I seem to languish.
. . . Meanwhile I shall pass my time with Grocyn, Lin-
acre and our friend Lily: the first of whom is, as you
know, the only director of my life in your absence; the
second, the master of my studies, the third my most
dear companion. Farewell, and continue to love me as
you do.[139]

These are "good friends" in the Aristotelian sense. A sense
of the moment in history, affection one for the other, and a
willingness to support and defend each other animated this
group of friends. But an additional characteristic seems worthy of consideration. There seems in each of them not only
a friendship for each other but a commitment to a higher
cause. In their cases, the cause is the new learning put to use
in furtherance of the cause of Christ and his Church. Drawn
together by their mutual respect, and animated by a shared
vision, they were able to influence the world they lived in,
and beyond. "The glory of Colet, Erasmus and More is that
they maintained undimmed throughout their careers their
ideal of the Church of Christ as a Catholic Society that no
plausible combination of self-interest with the hope of success for their schemes could have availed to detach them
from that Catholic unity."[140] This shared understanding
mirrors and merges with Fisher's: "[Fisher] was among the
few to recognize the importance of learning to a progressive
understanding of man and his place in the world. He knew
that much [reform] needed to be done, but it never occurred
to him to question the supreme importance of the Church
as the living center of the religious life of the people."[141]

Fisher's circle was tighter, circumscribed as it was by his ministerial and administrative duties, as well his introverted personality. Yet his affection for his fellow man under God is reflected in a prayer he composed:

> Thy strict commandment is that I should love thee with all my heart, with all my soul, with all my mind, with all my power. And this, I know, I do not, but am full far short and wide therefrom, which thing I perceive by the other loves that I have had of thy creatures heretofore. For such as I sincerely loved, I loved them so that I seldom did forget them. They were ever in my remembrance and almost continually mine heart was occupied with them and my thought ran ever upon them as well absent as present. Specially when they were absent I much desired to have their presence and to be there where they were, or else my heart were never in rightful quiety.[142]

While Erasmus, and to a lesser extent Thomas More and others, were effusive in their descriptions of friendship, Fisher prefers to go straight to the source: Jesus's great commandment in Matthew 22:36–40.

Thomas More was indeed born and made for friendship. His willingness to acquire and maintain friends, his discernment concerning which friends to continue associating with, his insistence on high character, his attention to their (sometimes demanding) needs, and his "kindness and sweetness of temper" toward them make for worthy consideration. However, there is a consideration beyond that of Erasmus that merits further reflection.

Because of More's broad-mindedness concerning the
things of earth and his constant contemplation of the things
of God, his understanding of friendship encompassed a
vision of eternity. He foresaw friendship in heaven with his
persecutors on earth. He understood, as C. S. Lewis did,
that one has never talked to a mere mortal:

> It is a serious thing to live in a society of possible gods
> and goddesses, to remember that the dullest most
> uninteresting person you can talk to may one day
> be a creature which, if you saw it now, you would be
> strongly tempted to worship, or else a horror and a
> corruption such as you now meet, if at all, only in a
> nightmare. . . . You have never talked to a mere mortal.
> Nations, cultures, art, civilizations—these are mortal,
> and their life is to ours as the life of a gnat. But it
> is immortals whom we joke with, work with, marry,
> snub, and exploit—immortal horrors or everlasting
> splendors.[143]

This eternal vision affected the way More treated even those
we would call his "enemies." His friendship with King
Henry VIII is a prime example. The king and More were
indeed close friends before Henry's great matter arose. More
first introduced Erasmus to King Henry VIII in 1499 when
they visited King Henry VII's children at the royal palace.
The future Henry VIII was then nine years old. They would
meet again some twenty years later, and for the next twenty
years, they enjoyed a close friendship. Bosset describes the
tragic tale of lost friendship this way:

> More's greatest act of charity [was] his love for the
> King. How hard it is to recall a parallel friendship in
> history. Here is the story of a scholar and saint, a man
> of European reputation, who was ready to sacrifice
> both convenience and career not only for the sake of
> his country but from a deep and lasting affection for
> the King. That More could read Henry through and
> through and yet allow the King to triumph over him is
> the final proof of his extraordinary charity. More loved
> Henry, and the King, in a brittle, self-centered way,
> returned this love.[144]

Knowing how the story ends, it seems impossible to consider the mutual affection that existed for decades. For his
part, before he succumbed to his excessive dependence on
flattery, his obsessive concern for an heir, his moral and
sexual depravity, and his ultimate tyrannical execution of
those with whom he disagreed, King Henry was very fond
of Thomas More. He shared his humor, laughed at his jokes,
and enjoyed his company. He even went so far as to issue a
direction that required More to be almost constantly present
at court. And before the great falling out, Henry, Catherine
of Aragon, and More enjoyed frequent private moments of
friendship together. The king was known to pay "surprise"
visits to More at his Chelsea home, to play with his children,
and to walk with More in his gardens. To the king, More
was an "old and devoted friend."[145] Thus, More truly was
executed by a friend, making this a tragic tale of a torn and
tattered friendship.

But for More's part, he never lost his love for his friend. It is only when we grasp this point that his conduct under imprisonment, and to the very point of death, is fully understood. He worried about becoming lord chancellor until he got Henry's commitment that, on his great matter, he should look to God first, and after God, then to him. He also recognized the king's limitations, indicating to his son-in-law Roper that if his head could win Henry a castle in France, it would surely go. More's love for the king, while never failing, was tempered by his understanding that "the friendships of this wretched world" are fickle.[146]

In his letters from prison to Meg, More repeatedly intones the king's kindness to him. If it were possible to take the oath and not offend God, he would, for he was bound to the king for "his most singular bounty, many ways shown and declared."[147] And he prayed that God would "incline the noble heart of the king's highness to the tender favor of you all, and to favor me no better than God and myself know that my faithful heart toward him and my daily prayer for him do deserve."[148]

Over the course of repeated interrogations, More insisted that the king had been kind to him. When first summoned to answer the Bill of Attainder, More readily admitted to Cromwell and others the king's "manifold benefits and bountiful goodness most benignly bestowed" upon him.[149] At his trial, having eviscerated Richard Rich for his perjury, and the court for its refusal to acknowledge the element of malice in the Act of Treason, he turned his attention back to the love and respect he had received from his majesty, the king:

Besides this, the manifold goodness of the king's highness himself, that has been so many ways my singular good lord, and gracious sovereign, and that has
so dearly loved and trusted me, even at my very first
coming into his noble service, with the dignity of his
honorable Privy Council vouchsafing to admit me,
and to offices of great credit and worship most liber-
ally advanced me; and finally with that weighty room
of his grace's high chancellor, the like whereof he never
did to temporal man before, next to his own royal
person, the highest officer in this whole realm, so far
above my qualities or merits able and meet thereof of
his own incomparable benignity honored and exalted
me; by the space of twenty years and more showing
his continual favor toward me, and (until at mine own
poor suit it pleased his highness giving me license with
his majesty's favor to bestow the residue of my life,
for the provision of my soul, in the service of God,
and of his special goodness thereof to discharge and
unburden me) most benignly heaped honors continually more and more upon me: all this his highness'
goodness, I say, so long thus bountifully extended
towards me, were in my mind, my lords, matters sufficient to convince this slanderous surmise by this man
so wrongfully imagined against me.[150]

In addition to constituting marvelous advocacy, this lengthy
oration indicates More's grateful heart, humble soul, and
appreciation for a sustained friendship.

To yet another, on the day of his execution, he told his jailor:

> I have always been much bound to the king's highness for the benefits and honors that he had still from time to time most bountifully heaped upon me; and yet more bounden am I to his grace for putting me into this place, where I have had convenient time and space to have remembrance of my end. And so help me God, most of all Master Pope, am I bound to his highness that it pleases him so shortly to rid me out of the miseries of this wretched world, and therefore will I not fail earnestly to pray for his grace both here, and also in the world to come.[151]

These repeated pronouncements of gratitude given to disparate people over a considerable period of time reflect a consistent attitude of gratitude and an appreciation of a friendship bestowed.

And, of course, at the point of death, he returns to the counsel the king had once given that More turn first to God, and after God, to him. Recalling that advice, More dies with these words on his lips: "I die the King's good servant, and God's first." Many acknowledge the concept of "servant leadership," the notion that any effective leader must put the concerns of his followers ahead of his own convenience. More lived a life of "servant friendship."

The law admits the dying declarations of an unavailable witness presuming them to be true.[152] Thomas More's expressions of friendship and gratitude to King Henry VIII at the point of death are either the words of an epic deceiver, an utterly unstable dissembler, or the very words of truth from a virtuous friend.

That they are the latter is confirmed by his expressions of friendship with the judges following his sentence: "I verily trust and shall therefore right heartily pray, that though your lordships have now here in earth been judges to my condemnation, we may yet hereafter in heaven merrily all meet together to our everlasting salvation." And written in his prayer book in his hand, this request for grace:

> To think my greatest enemies my best friends
> For the brethren of Joseph could never have done
>   him
> So much good with their love and favor
> As they did him with their malice and hatred.[153]

Such love. Such virtuous friendship. We must amend Erasmus's description. Thomas More was born and made *and died* for friendship.

CHAPTER 8

Baptist

"His name is John."

Names are fascinating.
God has over two-hundred of them mentioned in the Bible, each representing a different characteristic of the Almighty One. To name someone conveys identity, a sense of place, and sometimes a sense of purpose. We often name children after saints or ancestors intending in doing so to accomplish the twofold purpose of honoring the past and inspiring the future. Biblical significance is attached to naming. Jesus, Abraham, Paul, and the subject of this chapter, John the Baptist, were named or renamed as part of their prophetic roles. The act of naming is an awesome yet under-appreciated power.

The name John means "Yahweh is gracious." It is the name of twenty-three popes, eight Byzantine emperors, and many former rulers of England, France, Sweden, Denmark, Poland, Portugal, Bulgaria, Russia, and Hungary.

John Fisher was born in Beverly, England—named after St. John Beverly.[154] He was baptized at the church of St. John the Evangelist. And he lived a life of devotion to St. John the

Baptist, which would take imitative shape in a remarkable way, as we shall see.

In the first reading for the Solemnity of the Nativity of Saint John the Baptist,[155] we read in Isaiah 49: "Hear me, O coastlands, listen, O distant peoples. The LORD called me from birth, from my mother's womb he gave me my name."

The story is a familiar one. Voiceless Zachariah, eight days after the birth of John the Baptist, scribbled for all to see, "His name is John." While this seems simple enough to us, it was not a family name, and this shocked those who witnessed the naming. His son's name was given to his wife, Elizabeth, by an angel while his son resided in her womb. Zachariah's son, John, would become the voice of a herald, the voice that proclaimed repentance and preparation for the kingdom of heaven, and which reflected utmost humility before the Savior whose sandals he felt unworthy to fasten. This voice would one day be silenced by Herod Antipas's wicked act in derogation of marriage. But not truly silenced, for it reverberates down through the ages, including into the sixteenth century, when it would resonate in the heart of another John.

John Fisher had a special devotion to John the Baptist. He maintained on his altar where he celebrated Mass a skull reminiscent of the Baptist's severed head, and he had an image of the Baptist in his library in Rochester, one of the "valuables" seized and destroyed by the crown when Fisher was imprisoned in the Tower. Thomas More replenished that image—knowing the depth of Fisher's devotion to John the Baptist. That devotion offers clues to Fisher's personality.

It is in many ways difficult for the modern man, even the modern Christian man, to identify with the character of John the Baptist. Our minds recoil from his asceticism, the fasting, the austerity. It rejects the lack of ambition, finds off-putting the instinct to retreat into the dessert, to eat locust and honey, to wear camel hair and leather belts, to be impervious to human respect. The Baptist comes at us with formidable words of challenge, exhorting repentance: "For the kingdom of heaven is at hand." Repentance—that's the Good News? Would that he be less confrontational, more accepting, more tolerant.

Fisher fits the Baptist's profile: unyielding discipline, unshakeable will, and untiring patience.[156] Discipline, will, and patience, these things are foreign to the modern mind so programmed to the pursuit of comfort, acclaim, and immediate gratification. It prefers a camel hair blazer to the real thing. In this setting, God's kingdom fights for attention. Usually, the lust of the flesh and the eyes, and the pride of life, gets the better of the fight. To win us anew, God from time to time sends messengers who cry "Stop! There is One greater among us. Look and see." It may take a Baptist or a Fisher to get our attention, to declare truth to power, to bring us back. The authenticity of such a person is itself an attention grabber, simultaneously haunting, challenging, and inexplicable, but also fascinating and attractive. What could possibly explain such behavior?

Fisher was a sixteenth-century John the Baptist, unconsciously so at first. But caught in the web of palace deceit and attacks on the Church, he became more keenly aware of the identification. The ascetic bishop couldn't care less what others thought of him. Whereas More was a Renaissance man before the Renaissance was, Fisher frequently fasted and worked alone in a cold library where he prepared sermons for the salvation of souls.[157] He survived an assassination attempt by food poisoning, because he was, of course, fasting. His servant who cleared the table and nibbled on what Fisher left behind was not so lucky.

The similarities between the two Johns are striking. For one, their day jobs were quite different than the issue that brought them into conflict with kings. John the Baptist was the herald, the one who from his mother's womb made known the presence of Jesus. "For behold, when the voice of your greeting came to my ears, the child in my womb leaped for joy" (Lk 1:44). His vocation was to baptize (hence the moniker)—the baptism of repentance, to preach the necessity of preparing for the kingdom of heaven, to be the prophet of the Most High.

Since the age of thirty-five, Fisher was chancellor of Cambridge, re-elected yearly until after ten years he was named chancellor for life. He was appointed bishop of Rochester by Henry VII, and his intellectual excellence and virtue caused Henry VIII in an earlier time to boast of Fisher's incomparable virtue and learning. Pope Paul III made Fisher a cardinal.[158] But placed on a scale and weighed against the king's lust, it mattered not.

Fisher's self-understanding of walking in the footsteps of John the Baptist was intense. As we have noted, he said Mass with a Baptist skull on his altar.[159] This was confirmed when Henry's commissioners looking to seize the property of the arrested bishop inventoried his possessions. Among the few items seized was "a St. John's head standing at the end of the altar."[160] It seems that Bishop Fisher kept ever before him "this emblem of royal tyranny and saintly consistency."[161]

Fisher's intense interest in the Baptist was not limited to imagery and devotional skulls. His writings reflect a conscious awareness of the role of the ascetic, prophetic, heralding mission of the Baptist. In the section on marriage in Fisher's treatise concerning Henry VIII's *Defense of the Seven Sacraments* (allegedly written with the assistance of Thomas More), Fisher described the death of John the Baptist as a powerful witness to the sanctity of marriage. For if it were not such a grave matter, John would have focused his judgement on Herod's other sinful activity rather than his adulterous relationship with Herodias. Even before Henry started acting like Herod, Fisher was influenced by the Baptist.

It was the papal legatine hearing, though, that sealed Fisher's fate as previously discussed. His courageous "No sir, not I" to Henry's asserted claim that he had the theological support of all the bishops of the realm enraged the king. But what really drew his ire was Fisher's direct link of Henry to Herod and Fisher to John the Baptist. Fisher brings the similarity into unavoidable relief at the hearing in 1529. In defending the legitimacy of the marriage of Henry and Catherine, Fisher indicated his willingness to die in defense of the marriage just as John the Baptist had laid down his life under similar circumstances, for that saint "regarded it as impossible for him to die more gloriously than in the cause of marriage."[162] Henry was stung by Fisher's reference to John the Baptist. His counselor, Gardiner, derisively demanded by what token had the king deserved to be likened to Herod?

And by what right did the bishop of Rochester liken himself to John the Baptist, rashly declaring that he had a more just cause to sustain than the Baptist himself? If Fisher had in Henry's mind drawn a line in the sand when he denied signing an affidavit in support of Henry's theological position, he jumped across that line with two feet in drawing the parallel to John the Baptist.

But was Fisher's comparison not apt? Herod, after divorcing his wife Phaseaelis, had taken Herodias, his brother Phillip's divorced wife, as his own. His friend, John, instructed him that such a move was not lawful, that his conduct imperiled his soul, that he needed to repent. Initially, Herod "heard him gladly," even though he was "perplexed," for John was "a righteous and holy man."[163] But Herodias would have none of it. Ultimately, Herod had John bound and imprisoned "for the sake of Herodias."[164] Perhaps that was all he intended to do, that is, until Salome, the daughter of Herodias, captivated him with her lewd banquet dance and, for her reward and at her mother's request, demanded "the head of John the Baptist here on a platter." Snared in the lust of the flesh, the lust of the eyes, and the pride of life, Herod could not refuse her. John's mere presence, even hidden away in a prison cell, could not be tolerated. He must be beheaded at his paramour's request.

Fisher's parallel to the Baptist is strong: his name; his ascetic, austere, prophetic ministry; his call to repentance in his sermons; his witness at the legatine council; and more than anything, his stated willingness to die in defense of a proper understanding of marriage. And die he did when his uncompromising message to the king caused envy and hatred in his paramour, and ultimately resulted in a vengeful beheading.

John the Baptist and John are mirror images. Whereas Herod had been consumed by lust for his brother Phillip's wife, Henry VIII's lust consumed him with a passion for getting rid of his brother Arthur's wife. He would have Anne Boleyn at any cost. Her desire to be queen and her coy resistance to the king's advances, demanding first a ring and a crown, ultimately overpowered Henry's conscience. As Shakespeare would later note, "His conscience crept to close to another lady."[165] In this respect, Boleyn is a mirror image of Herodias. No one would stand in her way, not even the king's former tutor, counselor, and bishop. And in the wake of his execution, it is rumored that Anne Boleyn requested "the bishop's bleeding head brought before her in order to insult it."[166]

It is curious that there appears some sense of reluctance on behalf of the two despots. Herod reacted with distress at the request of Herodias's daughter for the head of the Baptist. But he complied in part "because of his oaths and his dinner guests."[167] He had staked himself out with a promise under oath: "Ask me anything you want. . . . I will give you up to half my kingdom."[168] Afterward, in his confusion, he would say in response to rumors about Jesus's resurrection, "John whom I beheaded, has been raised from the dead." Likewise, when the news of Thomas More's execution reached the ears of King Henry VIII while he sat at a dice game, he sprang up, pointed at Anne Boleyn, and shouted, "You are responsible." More's prophetic poem about Herod's act of beheading John the Baptist is recreated here:

Such dainty dishes grace the board of Kings
Believe me, poor men do not eat such things.

Scholar H. Daniel-Rops notes, "The blood of this new John the Baptist was soon to spill over the Tudor Herodias. A year later to the very day, she too would mount the scaffold steps." [169]

One final parallel. John the Baptist's ascetic life, prophetic preaching, and powerful magnetism had people in his day questioning whether he was Elijah incarnate. They would have remembered the words of Isaiah: "A voice of one calling in the wilderness prepare the way for the Lord; make straight in the desert a highway for our God. . . . And the glory of the Lord will be revealed" (40:3–4). They may well have remembered Malachi's prophecy: "Behold, I will send you Elijah the prophet before the coming of the great and dreadful day of the Lord. And he will turn the hearts of the fathers to the children, and the hearts of the children to their fathers, lest I come and strike the earth with a curse."

Strike he did. Henry VIII"s wanton lust and thirst for power resulted in a "strike that cursed the earth." And he interpreted the curse not in a way that would regulate his passions but rather justify them. God cursed him, he alleged, with the lack of a male heir because of his unbiblical marriage (but apparently not because of his serial affairs). Some would think that his reconsidered view of his voluntary union with Catherine would lead to repentance and penance, perhaps in the form of consecrated celibacy or a quiet, prayerful retreat. But this is not what he had in mind.

In his violent execution of a plan to marry again, and to foster an heir, this time with a younger woman with whom he was smitten, he would demand compliance. Compliance of thought, word, and deed. It was inevitable that this approach would run headlong into Fisher's commitment to "true truth," not the "truth" convenient to the king. Fisher would not budge. For he had "taken great pains to arrive at the truth and he would not change his mind without injury to both his reputation and his conscience."[170] The King had power over his body; Fisher retained exclusive control over his soul. He would not yield.

In this contest between unchecked passion on the king's side and unwavering commitment to truth on Fisher's, the sovereign would lose. Once known as the "Defender of the Faith" for his writings in support of the sacraments, he was now on a road to perdition. Hearts were turned away. Children and fathers turned not to each other but against each other. Henry would execute the man his father had named a bishop, and his grandmother had named her chaplain. He would disinherit his daughter Mary, whom he had with Catherine, and produce a daughter Elizabeth with Anne Boleyn and a son Edward with Jane Seymour.

They in turn would spend their adult lives sparring, warring, and striving against each other. Following his father's death, Edward VI would assume the throne at a young age and would govern a nation in turmoil as a regent king. Nearing death, he would repudiate the will of his father Henry VIII in an unsuccessful attempt to prevent his Catholic older sister from obtaining the throne. Despite that effort, Mary would become queen but prove to be unpopular and would, among other disfavored things, marry the son of Catherine of Aragon's nephew. She imprisoned her sister Elizabeth in a vain attempt to retain the throne. Her aggressive prosecution of "dissenters" earned her the epitaph "Bloody Mary." She would bear no heir but instead be replaced by Elizabeth. Throughout her reign, Elizabeth perceived her first cousin once removed, Mary Queen of Scots, as a threat, and had her imprisoned for eighteen years, before she was ultimately beheaded. Tudor England would suffer one religious conflict after another for a hundred years. Henry VIII's children's reigns would be marked by chaos, confusion, and disorder. English soil would be turned red by the deaths of Catholic and Protestant martyrs. The apples had not fallen far from the Henrician tree.

Fisher, standing in the power and tradition of Elijah and John the Baptist in his day, foresaw all this and spoke against it. "'But I tell you that Elijah has already come, and they did not recognize him, but did to him whatever they pleased. So also the Son of Man will certainly suffer at their hands.' Then the disciples understood that he was speaking to them of John the Baptist." Like John the Baptist, Fisher was a suffering prophet, unrecognized by the dominant forces of his day who did to him whatever they pleased. And reaped the whirlwind of calamity their ignoble behavior caused.

The personalities of the cosmopolitan More and the ascetic Fisher could not have stood in greater contrast. More is called an angel for his sweetness, wit, and wisdom. Yet Fisher is likened to John the Baptist, of whom our Lord proclaimed, "Among those born of women there has arisen no one greater." Pretty high praise, from a pretty high source. It is worth pondering why that is so.

CHAPTER 9

Detachment

"The field is won."

In June of 1520, years before the central events of this narrative, King Henry VIII, with the assistance of Cardinal
Wolsey, pulled off a spectacular meeting of kings near Calais, the only English held property on the European continent. Its ostentatious display of power and wealth earned it
the name "The Field of the Cloth of Gold." The purpose of
the meeting was to demonstrate to the world, and to each
other, the wealth, power, and magnificence of the kingdoms
of France and England, and their respective young, dashing,
and powerful kings. The end game, and hopeless hope, was
that peace might be inspired through exhibitions of strength.

The meeting proved to be an unmitigated disaster and was
described by one historian as "the most portentous decep-
tion on record." Before and after the gathering of the self-de-
clared peace-seeking kings from England and France, King
Henry VIII sabotaged the event by meeting separately with
the Holy Roman emperor, Charles V, to conspire against
France. War would soon resume to the great detriment of
the citizens of the respective countries.

But the weeks-long event outside Calais was *temporally* magnificent. Each king tried to outshine the other, with dazzling tents and spectacular clothing, feats of athletic prowess, huge feasts, music, jousting, and games. The tents and the costumes displayed cloths made of gold and expensive fabric woven with silk and gold thread

Both More and Fisher attended the meeting, More as a member of the king's court and Fisher as part of his entourage, which included nearly four thousand people and over two thousand horses. More than 2,200 sheep were consumed in the three-week period, and more than 2,800 tents provided the backdrop to the dazzling temporary structures built for the kings on adjacent hills.

Although he attended the Field of the Cloth of Gold meeting, More left no description. It surely provided the inspiration for his later comment to his son-in-law Roper when the latter complimented him on his friendship with Henry: "I thank our Lord, son. I find his grace my very good lord indeed, and I believe he does as singularly favor me, as any subject within this realm. Howbeit, son Roper, I may tell thee, I have no cause to be proud thereof, for if my head would win him a castle in France, it should not fail to go."[171]

Fisher, on the other hand, delivered a sermon later that year on the feast of All Saints in which he described the scene at length:

> Our eyes have seen many pleasures, many gay sights, many wonderful things that have appeared and seemed unto us joyous and comfortable. But yet all these were but counterfeits of the true joys, all these

were but dull and dark images of the perfect comfort which the blessed saints have now above in the kingdom of heaven. I doubt not but ye have heard of many goodly sights which were showed of late beyond the sea, with much joy and pleasure worldly. Was it not a great thing within so short a space to see three great Princes of this world? I mean the Emperor, and the king our master, and the French king. And each of these three in so great honor, showing their royalty, showing their riches, showing their power with each of their noblesse appointed and appareled in rich clothes, in silks, in velvets, cloths of gold and such other precious arraignments. To see three right excellent Queens at once together, and of three great realms. That one, the noble Queen our mistress, the very exemplar of virtue and nobleness to all women. And unto Louis French king, sister to our sovereign lord, a right excellent fair Lady. And every one of them accompanied with so many other fair ladies in sumptuous and gorgeous apparel, such dancings, such harmonies (music), such dalliance, and so many pleasant pastimes, so curious houses and buildings, so preciously appareled, such costly welfare of dinners, suppers and banquets, so delicate wines, so precious meats, such and so many noble men of arms, so rich and goodly tents, such joustings, such tourneys, and such feats of war. These were assuredly wonderful sights as for this world, and as much as hath been read of in years done, or in any Chronicles or Histories heretofore written, and as great as men's wits and studies could devise and imagine for that season.[172]

Having described the sumptuous affair in detail, Fisher drew a quite different conclusion from the one King Henry VIII intended to convey. First, that the joys and pleasures of this life, "be they never so great," have a weariness to them. "There is no meat nor drink so delicate so pleasant, so delectable but if a man or a woman be long accustomed therewith he shall have at the length a loathsomeness thereof."[173] After a while, Fisher remarked, many of the retinue wished they were at home. He lamented the expense of the affair, concluding that many men's coffers were emptied and "many were brought to a great ebb and poverty."[174] The extravagant exhibition of wealth turned others to pride, envy, and covetousness, many wishing they could own such marvelous clothes, jewelry, and horses, whereas before they were content with what they had.

Cosmic forces, God perhaps, conspired against the extravagant exhibition. Fisher ruefully observed:

> While we were there, sometimes there was such dust, and therewithal so great winds that all the air was full of dust. The gowns of velvet, and cloth of gold were full of dust, the rich trappers of horses were full of dust, hats, caps, gowns were full of dust and briefly to speak, horse and men were so encumbered with dust that scantly one might see another. The winds blew down many tents, shaked sore the houses that were built for pleasure. . . . Sometimes again we had rains

and thunders so ummeasureable that no man might
stir forth to see any pleasures."[175]

We who live on this side of a pandemic might readily concur
with Fisher's description of the vanity of such an affair. We
plan and build and strive for gain, and in an instant it can
all disappear. So what conclusions should be drawn from
this episode? Fisher concludes, "Kings and Emperors all be
but men, all be but mortal. All the gold and all the precious
stones of this world, can not make them but mortal men.
All the rich apparel that can be devised, can not take from
them the condition of mortality. They be in themselves but
earth and ashes, and to earth they must return, and all their
glory well considered and beholden with right eyes is but
very miserable."[176]

The Field of the Cloth of Gold is a metaphor for our lives.
What is needed is "right eyes" to perceive a vision of our
mortality. The worries and riches of the world, its urgencies,
its busyness, its demands on our time and attention, its dis-
tractions, tend to keep us off balance and out of touch with
eternal verities. One needs to direct his gaze up where the
things of earth pale in the view of heaven. The earth's fields
of cloth and gold dazzle and distract but do not satisfy.

Thomas More knew this. A decade after he experienced
the Field of Cloth of Gold, he found himself contemplating
another field—caught between the Charybdis of King Henry's demands and the Scylla of his own conscience. In 1534,
after the marriage of King Henry and Anne Boleyn, More
feared that his practice of studied silence on the king's great
matter would no longer keep him safe: "God give grace, that

these matters within a while not be confirmed with oaths," he exclaimed to his son-in-law.

But soon after he expressed that fear, the Succession Act was passed. In addition to legitimizing any forthcoming off-spring of Henry with Anne Boleyn, it indeed provided for a subsequent oath requiring, among other things, affirmation of Henry's version of the facts surrounding the marriage of Catherine and Arthur: the annulment, the power (or lack thereof) of the pope, and the (newly discovered) supremacy of the ministers of the Church of England. It also forbade the "slandering" of the king's marriage to Queen Anne. A theo-logical understanding contrary to Henry's was disallowed. Infringement on this act by word or deed constituted high treason and was to be punished by forfeiture of property and death. Those who were found to have spoken against the crown "but did not go further," or "who obstinately refused" to take the oath, were subject to forfeiture and imprison-ment "at the King's pleasure."[177]

At the time this act was being negotiated between the crown and Parliament, More had quietly retired to his home in Chelsea. Despite this retreat from public and political life, More became the first layman summoned to appear at Lambeth Castle to answer questions about his view of the act and to sign the inchoate oath. Receipt of the summons caused great trepidation among his family members. More responded as he always did before dealing with any weighty matters. He went to the chapel to pray, to confess, and to hear Mass. He then bade his family farewell and travelled to his interrogation by boat with his son-in-law Roper. As he got into the boat, More seemed grave. Suddenly, he "rounded me in the ear" and said, "Son Roper, the field is won."[178]

Roper had no idea what More meant by this odd phrase, but the dramatic change in mood made a lasting impression. He later reflected that "it was for the love of God wrought in him so effectually that it conquered all his carnal affections utterly."[179]

Roper may have come to this subsequent understanding of More's detachment by reflecting upon an earlier event. It was Roper and More again in a boat, this time going back to Chelsea after More first appeared before the king's commissioners having been attainted for misprision of treason. In a later chapter we will consider the lack of due process in this first of many attacks on the good name of More. What interests us here is More's attitude under examination as revealed to Roper. The anxious Roper asked More how the meeting went. More seemed unexpectedly "merry," which at first glance caused Roper to believe More may have been removed from the Bill of Attainder. But no, More revealed that it never occurred to him to bring it up: "By my truth son Roper, I never remembered it. . . . Will thou know son Roper why I was so merry? . . . In good faith I rejoiced son, that I had given the devil a foul fall, and that with those lords, I had gone so far as without great shame I could never go back again."

To reach the point of no return, to realize the field is won, the field of the cloth of gold put aside, More had found peace through detachment from the things of this world, even the good things of family, friends, and all the accomplishments that a diligent pursuit of virtue had wrought. This laudable exchange—the cares of the world for the cares of God, the things that you cannot keep for the love you cannot lose— gave him such peace he seemed in the moment joyful; joyful as he began the journey that led to his execution, now perceived by him to be the gateway to eternity. Fisher's conclusion that all is dust and ashes became More's life principle. His subsequent display of strength, courage, and peace in the persecution to follow flow out of this detachment.

Detachment enabled More to live consistently with his principles. Indeed, Pope St. John Paul II cites it as a ground for declaring More heavenly patron of statesmen and politicians: "His profound detachment from honors and wealth, his serene and joyful humility, his balanced knowledge of human nature and of the vanity of success, his certainty of judgement rooted in faith: these all gave him that confident inner strength that sustained him in adversity and in the face of death."[180]

Detachment and the sense of the vanity of success manifest in many ways, but one additional scene stands out with More. Soon after his discharge as the lord chancellor, More retired to Chelsea with a diminished income and serious concerns about the manner in which he would support his family. He foresaw tough times ahead, even short of the persecution to follow. He soon began to place his servants and workmen with other families, noblemen, and bishops. He then directed his attention to his own extended family then living with him. He expressed a desire to live together. But to do that, they must all chip in, and they must rethink their collective position in life going forward.

He approached the task indirectly by reciting his career history, and his remuneration over time as prelude to his admonition that they would now have to cut back: "I have been brought up at Oxford, at an Inn of Chancery, at Lincoln's Inn, and also in the king's court, and so forth from the lowest degree to the highest, and yet have I in yearly revenue at this present left me little above a hundred pounds by the year. So that now we must hereafter, if we like to live together, be contented to become contributories together."[181]

Having sought their advice on how to proceed and having received none, he then stated his own:

> But by my counsel it shall not be best for us to fall to the lowest fare first; we will not, therefore, descend to Oxford fare, nor to the fare of New Inn, but we will begin with Lincoln's Inn diet, where many, right-worshipful and of good years, do live full well. Which, if we find not ourselves the first year able to maintain, then we will the next year go one step down to New Inn fare, wherewith many an honest man is well contented. If that exceed our ability too, then will we, the next year descend to Oxford fare, where many grave, learned and ancient fathers be continually conversant. Which, if our ability stretch not to maintain neither; then may we yet, with bags and wallets, go a-begging together; and hoping that for pity some good folks will give us their charity at every man's door to sing *Salve Regina* and so to keep company and be merry together.[182]

More's fall from the king's grace created yet another opportunity to exhibit his detached persona. He habitually sung in the Church choir, although if all we knew about More was his choir performances, no book would ever be written. Even so, when he sang in the choir loft, Lady More sat alone. And as befits a man of such rank, at the conclusion of Mass, an aide would be dispatched to escort the lord chancellor's lady out of Church. The Sunday after his resignation, More, cap in hand, approached Lady More and said, "May it please your Ladyship to come forth now my Lord is gone." This self-deprecating act was one with More's humility. "He relished his fall from power as a blessed release from the perils of pride and worldliness and thus as an act of saving grace."[183]

The detached life which More absorbed over time seemed to be acquired naturally by John Fisher. Described as austere and ascetic by his friends, he cared little for the things of the world, except for his world class library, "his one extravagance,"[184] which was the envy of European scholars and the object of eventual total annihilation at the hands of Henry's rage. He became a priest at such a young age that he needed a dispensation to take orders. Having turned his back on the pleasantries and challenges of family life through the taking of orders at a young age, he continued in his life of study, self-discipline, and inner devotion to God. He was known for his "unyielding discipline," "unshakable will," and "untiring patience."[185]

Fisher ate little and slept on a pallet. He spent his hours in study, writing and preparing sermons in an unheated library. His foreign travel was non-existent, except for the one trip outside England to the Field of Cloth of Gold. He fasted frequently and with such rigor that he suffered poor health from an early age and possessed gaunt features. His asceticism formed his character and once saved his life, as we noted earlier but is worth mentioning again. Shortly after his public stand against the king's divorce, an attempt by poisoning was made on his life. Sadly, his cook died. But Fisher survived—as a result of his most recent fast, he did not eat the addled soup.

Fisher was simply a holy man. Fr. Vincent McNabb, an Irish-born Dominican biographer, describes him in this way: "There used to be a phrase which gave 'the English Way' in matters of holiness, to wit: 'Garden of the Soul Catholic.' In reading what his biographer tells of the holiness of Fisher we can hardly help recalling the phrase. Grafted upon a character that was sturdy almost to the point of severity, this holiness was in the common ways of Catholic life."[186]

This holiness comprised three elements:

- the frequent and reverent saying of Holy Mass "always with devotion and with a (John the Baptist) skull placed on the altar,"
- the praying of his Breviary faithfully, with a "reverence to the holy name of Jesus,"
- and bodily mortification, including fasting.

This seems to be the key to his devotional life, the cultivation of the garden Catholic, which enabled him to meet the great challenges to come.

Perhaps the best symbol of Bishop Fisher's detachment was his reaction to being made a cardinal. When told that the cardinal's red hat was on its way to England, Henry retorted, "Well, let the pope send him a hat, when he will. But I will so provide that, whensoever it comes, he shall wear it on his shoulders, for head shall he have none to see it on." Fisher's response to the same news was characteristic: he said that if the cardinal's hat were laid at his feet, he would not stoop to take it up.[187] In any event, Henry's irritation was not feigned. Fisher would be executed within a month of his being named a cardinal.

More and Fisher lived well because they cared less for the vanities of life. By righteous intention, disciplined living, and focus on the things above, they were ready when the moment came.

S. IOANNIS FISHER

Portrait of Bishop John Fisher, Gwyneth Thompson-Briggs (gwyneththompsonbriggs.com);
found in Our Lady of the Mountains Catholic Church, Jasper, GA

Portrait of Sir Thomas More (1478-1535) (oil on panel), after a painting by Holbein the Younger, Hans (1497/8-1543) / German, Bridgeman Images.

(*Above*) King Henry VIII (oil on canvas), after a painting by Holbein the Younger, Hans (1497/8-1543) / German, Bridgeman Images

(*Below*) (*Left*) Catherine of Aragon, Queen of England from 1509 until 1533 as the first wife of King Henry VIII, 1520 (oil on oak panel), English School, (16th century) / English, Photo © Stefano Baldini / Bridgeman Images. (*Right*) Anne Boleyn (1507-36); second wife of Henry VIII; 1534 (oil on panel), English School, (16th century) / English, Bridgeman Images

(*Above*) (*Left*) Cardinal Thomas Wolsey (c.1475-1530) advisor and Chancellor to King Henry VIII and Bishop of Wells. (oil on panel), Strong, Sampson (c.1550-1611) / British, © Colchester & Ipswich Museums Service / Bridgeman Images. (*Right*) Lord Cromwell, Wearing the Order of St George, Holbein, Hans (1497/8-1543) (school of) / German, Bridgeman Images.

(*Below*) (*Left*) Richard Rich, First Baron Rich (c.1496-1567) engraved by Francesco Bartolozzi (1727-1815) (engraving), The Stapleton Collection / Bridgeman Images. (*Right*) John the Baptist, detail from the Ghent Altarpiece, 1432 (oil on panel), © Lukas - Art in Flanders VZW / Bridgeman Images

(*Above*) Statues of Sts. John Fisher and Thomas More flank the names of forty martyrs of the English Reformation. Church of Our Lady of Victories in Kensington, London. Photo used with permission.

(*Below*) Meeting at the Field of the Cloth of Gold, 7th June 1520, after Hans Holbein the Elder (1460/5-1524) (oil on canvas), Bridgeman Images

(*Above*) Portrait of Sir Thomas More and his Family, after a painting by Hans Holbein the Younger, 1590s (oil on canvas), Lockey, Rowland (c.1565-1616) / English, National Trust Photographic Library/John Hammond / Bridgeman Images

(*Above*) Beaufort House, Chelsea, England, where Sir Thomas More lived. Lebrecht Authors / Bridgeman Images

(*Below*) Tower of London, photograph by Alexander Chaikin/Shutterstock

(*Above*) Sir Thomas More and his daughter Margaret observing from his prison window the Carthusian Monks going to execution, 1535. Illustration from The Comprehensive History of England (Gresham Publishing, 1902), © Look and Learn / Bridgeman Images

(*Below*) The Martyrdom of the Carthusian Monks (engraving), English School, (17th century). Between 1535-37 groups of Carthusian monks from the London Charterhouse monastery were hung, drawn and quartered by order of the English government, under the influence of King Henry VIII and his break from the Catholic Church; Bridgeman Images

CHAPTER 10

Injustice

"For it is a very straight gate we are in."

In April of 1534, Bishop Fisher and Thomas More were summoned to Lambeth Palace to appear for interrogation by the king's men concerning his great matter. Thus began the final process that led inexorably to their execution more than a year later.

Both knew their fate. When warned by the Duke of Norfolk, *Indignatio principis mors est* ("The wrath of the king is death"), More responded, "Is that all my lord? Then in good faith is there no more difference between your grace and me but that I shall die today and you tomorrow?"[188] Upon being subpoenaed, More boarded a boat to journey from Chelsea to Lambeth. We have already examined his mental state in his comment to Roper, "The field is won."

Fisher likewise began a final journey from Rochester to London to respond to his summons. On horseback, bareheaded, already suffering from age and illness, almost blind, he rode erect, in the process encountering throngs of countrymen along the way. Many wept. To all, he raised his right hand in benediction. He seemed to possess an unfathomable serenity, as Michael Macklem points out: "He had made his choice and he was not afraid. The grief and anxiety he had suffered through long years of discouragement and defeat had now left him. He was more alone now than ever, but that no longer mattered. For five years he had labored to preserve the liberty of the English Church and he had failed. He had lost much, he had lost everything that mattered most to him. But he still possessed his soul in peace and this could not be taken away from him. It was enough."[189]

Upon being examined, both were ordered to the Tower. On the way, they encountered each other ironically at a gate known as the "Traitor's Gate." They had not seen each other in over a year. Embracing Fisher, More told him he hoped to see him in heaven. "This should be the way Sir Thomas," Fisher responded, "for it is a very straight gate we are in."[190]

The legal path to inevitable execution that each man journeyed toward is foreign to modern ears. The centuries of development of due process rights were virtually nonexistent then. Rights to representation, to an impartial jury, to an appeal, did not exist. It is hard for us, especially us lawyers, to imagine the lack of due process in Henrician England.

Perhaps it would be helpful to pause and reposition ourselves in modern times to consider what process More and Fisher might encounter if charged capitally today. And in this regard, the author's background as a former federal prosecutor and a current federal judge comes into play. For in past times, he has found himself standing before a jury asking its members to impose a capital sentence. And once, as a judge, he has pronounced those awful words, "May God have mercy on your soul" to a condemned man standing before him. Each time, his utterances were pronounced with fear and trembling, preceded and followed by deep reflection, meditation, and prayer. I shudder at the annihilating consequences of capital litigation involving a fellow human being.

Today, before anyone is condemned to death in federal court, a rigorous process is followed which is designed to provide as much due process as is humanly possible. The death penalty is no longer applicable to just any felony violation. It is used for the most aggravated of crimes. The accused cannot be questioned in police custody unless he is provided *Miranda* rights. If he is known to be represented by a lawyer in a matter, he may not be questioned at all about the crime without his lawyer being present. If he can't afford to retain counsel, the law mandates and assigns two attorneys experienced in capital litigation at tax payer expense. Before a federal prosecutor may present a capital charge to a grand jury, he must get approval from the attorney general of the United States. The defendant's attorneys have an opportunity to urge the attorney general to decline to authorize capital prosecution. If authorization is obtained and a grand jury returns a bill of indictment alleging a capital crime, the defendant is provided full discovery, usually in the form of an "open file" where the government provides access to all its evidence. Failure to comply with the rules requiring production of discovery may result in a dismissal of charges.

Once sufficient time for reviewing discovery and preparing for trial has passed, the jury is selected. The trial is "trifurcated" into parts: a guilt/innocence phase, a death qualifying stage, and an ultimate sentencing hearing. At each stage the burden is on the government to prove beyond a reasonable doubt the essential elements of the crime charged to the unanimous satisfaction of all twelve jurors. The lawyers for the government and defendant participate in a process to select an impartial jury. Jurors are struck for cause if they express an unyielding attitude in favor of, or against, imposition of the death penalty upon conviction. At the sentencing phase, the government must prove at least one aggravating factor beyond a reasonable doubt to the unanimous satisfaction of all twelve jurors. A defendant has the opportunity to prove mitigating factors by a preponderance of the evidence (the "more likely than not" standard). If one juror believes the mitigating factor(s) outweigh(s) the aggravating factor(s), or for any other reason she does not believe the death penalty is the appropriate sanction, it cannot be imposed. If the jury finds the death penalty for the accused, he is afforded appellate rights to the Circuit and eventually Supreme Court. This right of "direct appeal" is followed by habeas litigation up through those same tribunals. If a serious error is discovered in the process, the death penalty may be vacated or the trial remanded.

This scheme is subject of course to human error. But it is procedurally designed to safeguard against the wrongful conviction or sentencing of a capital defendant. As the Supreme Court has expressed in another context, "the twofold aim (of the law) is that [the] guilty shall not escape or innocence suffer."[191]

More's and Fisher's capital verdicts, in contradistinction to the modern scheme, were preordained. Although they were given process, it was not the process due. Their trials were show trials designed to give Henry what he wanted—their lives—with the appearance of justice. As More and Fisher met at the Traitor's Gate, they were encountering the full weight, and the full wrath, of the king's authority and the king's will.

While some have concluded that these trials comported with sixteenth-century standards of justice,[192] a close examination of some but not all the miscarriages of justice which occurred indicate the opposite—that these "trials" were unjust both procedurally and substantively. As More wrote, prophetically, in his play *The History of King Richard the Third*, "king's games" were like stage plays "for the more part played upon scaffolds."[193]

Bill of Attainder

The first remarkable aspect of their prosecutions was that both men were "attainted." A bill of attainder was an act of Parliament which declared a person guilty of a crime and punished him without a trial. It declared guilt and acted to deprive More and Fisher of liberty and other civil rights such as the right to own property.

This practice of attainder was considered so inconsistent with principles of justice and the right to trial that it was prohibited by the United States Constitution. Article 1, Section 9 of the United States Constitution forbids bills of attainder under federal law, and Section 10 forbids it under state law. Attainder was one of the grievances the early colonists alleged against the king of England, and they made sure to abolish it. Its flaws are obvious: the potential for abuse, the violation of due process, and under our constitutional scheme, the violation of the doctrine of the separation of powers. It should be the judicial branch, not the executive branch, that presides over a criminal trial and pronounces sentence.

John Fisher was first attainted for his involvement with an infamous person known as the "Nun of Kent" who had repeatedly prophesied the king's demise because of his divorce of Queen Catherine. More, the careful lawyer, had kept his distance from the nun and Parliament refused to attaint him on this ground. In fact, Henry tried three times to insert More's name in the Bill of Attainder, but Commons refused. Fisher's sentence was eventually remitted, but his and More's troubles were just beginning.

Around the time of Henry's (re)marriage to Anne Boleyn, More voiced a premonition to his son-in-law Roper, "God give grace son, that these matters within a while not be confirmed by oaths." His fears were soon realized. Parliament passed the first Act of Succession prohibiting any malicious slandering by writing, print, deed, or act of the king's title. This act was followed by an oath of allegiance not only to the succession but also to the legitimacy of the king's marriage to Anne, and concomitant illegitimacy of his prior marriage to Catherine. Neither More nor Fisher could in good conscience sign the oath. They were attainted in different bills in April, 1534, more than a year before their executions. From that point on, their home was a prison cell in the Tower of London, for failure to take the required oath constituted a misprision of treason and resulted in a life sentence "at the

King's good pleasure," the forfeiture of property, and the loss of the ability to pass on property.

Significantly, at this point in 1534, Henry had what he needed, but not what he wanted. More and Fisher were "legally dead." Neither man would set foot in free society again. And no jury was needed, no effort extended. From this point forward, they were separated from family, friends, and Church. The crown controlled their every movement. At one point, More would be deprived even of his books and his pens, only to be replaced by a stick of coal as his writing instrument. This horrible persecution should have ended here. But what the king wanted was utter annihilation, and his henchmen were just beginning.

Interrogations

While languishing in cold, damp cells in the Tower, each man getting older, both suffering from serious medical maladies and deprived of all human comfort, they were repeatedly interrogated by the king's counselors. We have already seen their chance meeting at Traitor's Gate where each was consigned to prison after interviews with the king's lord chancellor, secretary, and archbishop. The questioning would increase in frequency and intensity as desperate interrogators sought damaging answers that would satisfy Henry and justify execution.

Having resolved the issue of succession, the king ratcheted up his demands by pushing through two Acts of Parliament: the Act of Supremacy which declared the king Supreme Head of the Church of England, and an Act of

Treason. It was the latter act, the Act of Treason, which would be the basis for the trials of More and Fisher. Unlike the Act of Succession, this act had no required oath. It simply declared that "after the first day of February (1535)" any malicious "wish, will, or desire, by words or writing, or by craft" depriving the king's or queen's titles would constitute "high treason" punishable by execution. This act, the first of its kind that made the uttering of mere words treasonous, would then be applied to the imprisoned pair with a ferocity that was equally unprecedented. The interrogations of More and Fisher, already in jail for life on Bills of Attainder, would lead to the charges of treason that resulted in execution.

Henry's counselors bounced back and forth questioning the two men. More was interrogated on April 13 and 30, and June 2, 12, and 14. Fisher was examined on April 13, May 7, and June 12 and 14. Sometimes the examiners would tell one man that the other had capitulated in hopes of securing the cooperation of the one under examination.[194] Sometimes they would accuse both of conspiring because of the use of a common term, such as that the act represented a two-edged sword, "say either precisely with it [the statute] against my conscience to the loss of my soul, or precisely against it to the destruction of my body."[195] Although More never used the term "two-edged sword" when describing the interrogation to his daughter, Fisher did. The indictments would draw out the inference that the two collaborated, falsely putting that term in More's mouth as evidence of collusion with Fisher. The long period of incarceration on similar charges in the same Tower gave opportunity to the king's men to interrogate both in the hopes of getting damaging statements.

During that time, More and Fisher were not allowed to meet in person, but they were able to exchange letters through servants. These letters were burned and no actual evidence of their content was ever offered. But the exchange of letters allowed the inference of collusion. Finally, the convenience of incarceration in the Tower gave Richard Rich the opportunity to work his cunning against both men.

It is helpful in this regard to consider the law of conspiracy as it has developed over time, since the men were accused of conspiring or colluding with each other, and as in other ages up to our own, the crime of conspiracy or the accusation of collusion can be a rather amorphous thing.

A "conspiracy" is an agreement between two or more persons to join together to accomplish some unlawful purpose, what is sometimes called a "partnership in crime" in which each member agrees to commit a crime, knows the unlawful purpose of the agreement, and joins in willfully with the intent to further the unlawful purpose. At common law, there must also be proof of an overt act in furtherance of the conspiracy. But there is always the defense of being in the wrong place at the wrong time. Mere presence at the scene of an event, even with knowledge that a crime is being committed, or the mere fact that certain persons may have associated with each other, and may have assembled together and discussed common aims and interests, does not necessarily establish proof of the existence of a conspiracy. A person who has no knowledge of a conspiracy, but who happens to act in a way which advances some purpose of a conspiracy, does not thereby become a conspirator. Whether or not there is a criminal agreement or mere common interest or association is usually a question of fact for the jury, but it requires evidence upon which a reasonable jury could conclude a conspirator was guilty.

The strategy of the king's advisors was intended to wear down each man and *create* evidence where it otherwise did not exist. In Fisher's case, it worked. In More's, it was manufactured. Fisher was charged with denying the supremacy in an interrogation which occurred on June 12, 1535. More, meanwhile, was charged with maliciously remaining silent, conspiring in Fisher's treason, and affirmatively denying the king's supremacy. All of this occurred after being incarcerated for over a year and within a month of execution.

Lack of Discovery, Appeal

Modern day notions of discovery that avoid trial by ambush were not part of the process. More would be indicted on June 28, 1535 and tried two days later. Fisher similarly was indicted and tried within three days. Both men would learn of their charges after being dragged into court weak, in ill-health, and without counsel. Appeals? They did not exist. Summary execution of both men happened less than ten days after verdict.

Jury Composition

In sixteenth-century English jurisprudence, the concept of an impartial jury did not exist. Jurors were chosen, not disqualified, based upon personal knowledge of the facts in question. Even in light of this affront to an impartial jury, a bedrock of modern jurisprudence, More's jury constituted an absurd collection of souls and would lead to a fifteen-minute verdict. Five of them are described as follows: Sir Thomas Palmer was King Henry's dicing partner; Sir Thomas Spert was the clerk comptroller of the Royal Navy; Gregory Lovell and Geoffrey Chamber were minor courtiers, and John Parnell had once falsely accused then Judge More of accepting a bribe.

These deficiencies belie any notion that the trials were in any sense fair or just. They were show trials meant to give the king what he wanted with a veneer of respectability. One need look no further than this fact: On June 25, 1535, five days *before* More's trial, King Henry preemptively issued a "circular letter" which, among other things, asserted the king's title as Supreme Head of the Church of England. In that document, Henry ordered that public declarations be made of "the treasons, traitorously committed against us and our laws by the late bishop of Rochester and Sir Thomas More, knight, who thereby and by divers secret practices of the malicious minds against us intended to spread sedition."[196] Only after the publication of this circular pronouncing guilt did he form a special commission comprised of, among others, Anne Boleyn's uncle, brother, and father to indict, prosecute, and convict More. Proclamation of guilt first followed by indictment characterized the prosecution from beginning to end.

These deficiencies in the quest for justice are repugnant to all. But perhaps the most distasteful aspect of the show trials was the failure of the justice system to confine capital punishment, the ultimate punishment, to the language of the statute, and especially the element of malice expressly required therein. And to that deficiency, we turn now.

Malice

"Where there is no malice, there can be no offense."

I have often said that your perspective changes depending upon your seat in the courtroom (and I have sat in each of the judge's, prosecutor's, and defense counsel's chairs). A prosecutor believes that he is wearing a white hat representing the community in defending the good and prosecuting evil. But a defense lawyer sees a black hat when he looks across the aisle. It is he, the defense lawyer, who is championing freedom, defending the oppressed, and standing between the awful power of the state and his (at least presumed to be) innocent client. A judge sees himself as the expositor of the law, the one to whom jurors and parties look to for the "accurate application of the law and excellence in its expression."[197] Perhaps the remaining participants and observers listening to the legal speeches simply believe there are too many lawyers in the courtroom.

I say all this to make this point. The central issue in the trials of Fisher and More was the statutory requirement that the government prove that any words spoken by the defendant be done so "maliciously." The element of malice was read out of the statute at the trials in a way that led to certain convictions. And this certainty of conviction was the preordained result contemplated by all parties to the prosecution. And viewed from this perspective, the show trials, however legal they appeared, appear corrupt.

At the end of the day, and after all the legal wrangling, intense interrogation, and lengthy incarceration, the requirement of proving the legal element of "malice" still stood as a bulwark against injustice. The fact that it was made to disappear from the trials of both Fisher and More as an inconsequential, superfluous word is, from a jurisprudential perspective, deeply troubling. For if words do not matter, if men can adjust the meaning of words to suit their bloodlust, there is no justice.

That this would happen was anticipated from the outset: "that speaking is made high treason, which was never heard of before, that words should [be] high treason. But there was never such a sticking at the passing of any act in the lower house as was at the passing of the same [the November 1534 Act of Treason Concerning Supremacy], and that was the [word] "maliciously," which, when it was put, it was not worth [lacuna], for they would expound the same statute themselves at their pleasure."[198]

The Act of Treason made it a capital crime to maliciously deny the king's title, including that of Supreme Head of the Church of England. It is predicated on the notion of a malicious word or act. Secretary Cromwell's earlier efforts to make malicious spoken words treasonous had been unsuccessful. The Act of Succession limited that category of crime to misprision of treason, a non-capital offense. Thus, one could not be condemned for mere spoken words. But six months later, "maliciously" spoken words became high treason, meaning one was eligible for death if convicted in the Act of Treason. It was put into the act so that "a man might answer to the questions not maliciously, and be in no danger."[199] It was a safeguard against wrongful conviction. It had no other purpose.

This is so because the Act addressed "cancerous and traitorous hearts." It provided that:

> if any person or persons, after the first day of February (1535) next coming, do *maliciously* wish, will, or desire, by words or writing, or by craft imagine, invent, practice, or attempt any bodily harm to be done or committed to the King's most royal person, the Queen's, or their heirs apparent, or to deprive them or any of them of their dignity, title, or name of their royal estates, or slanderously and *maliciously* publish and pronounce by express writing or words, that the King our Sovereign Lord should be heretic, schismatic, tyrant, infidel, or usurper of the Crown [commits a capital offense.][200]

The Act goes on to enjoin "all true subjects" to eschew the "malicious intent" of traitors. The materiality of the term "malice" as an element of the offense reads across the ages with exquisite clarity. Malicious intent was needed to violate the Act of Treason.

So it was understood by the Commons. So it was understood by the king. When More was examined by Henry's counselors on June 3, they instructed him:

> That the king's Highness was nothing content nor sat-
> isfied with mine (earlier) answer, but thought that by
> my demeanor I had been occasion of much grudge and
> harm in the realm, and that I had an obstinate mind
> and an evil toward him, and that my duty was being
> his subject; and so he had them now in his name upon
> my allegiance to command me to make a plain and
> terminate answer whether I thought the statute law-
> ful or not, and that I should either acknowledge and
> confess it lawful that his Highness should be Supreme
> Head of the Church of England or else to utter plainly
> my malignity.[201]

According to the king's men, it was More's malignity that provoked the king and triggered the statute.

So it was understood by the Carthusian monks who were tried on June 11, 1535, just days before John Fisher's trial and less than a month before More's. The monk's joint defense to the charge of saying they would not consent to the king's title of "Supreme Head on Earth of the Church of England under Christ" was that they did not deny the title maliciously.

So it was understood by the Carthusian's jury who refused to condemn them "because their conscience persuaded them they did it 'not maliciously.'" The justices, who would also preside over the trials of More and Fisher, then instructed the jury that anyone who denied the supremacy did it mali-ciously and that the word "maliciously" in the statute was void. Notwithstanding this "directed verdict," the jury still would not condemn the holy men. Then Secretary Cromwell, "in a rage," went into the jury and threatened them. "And so being overcome by his threats, they found them guilty and had great thanks. But they were afterwards ashamed to show their faces and some of them took great thought for it."[202]

It should be noted that this construction given by the justices of the words of the statute departs from the common canons of interpretation used by judges. The first canon of interpretation violated is that a statute should be interpreted, if possible, so that the words used are not rendered superfluous.[203] But that is what the judge's instructions did—they rendered the term "maliciously" meaningless. The clear intent of the legislature by the deliberate insertion of the word "maliciously" was ignored, and the statute's meaning altered, by judicial fiat.

The second rule violated is the rule of lenity. In a criminal case, if a statute is ambiguous, meaning it is capable of two reasonable interpretations, the judge is required to construe the statute favorably to the accused. To the extent that there is ambiguity in the Act of Treason, that ambiguity should have been resolved in the favor of the monastic defendants. The Carthusians were condemned in the first instance by a vengeful royal demand; in the second, by a complicit legislative body; third, by a wrongful judicial construction; and fourth, by an intimidated jury. The king's wrath corrupted all it touched.

The wrongful Carthusian convictions were only the warm-up to the bloody summer of 1535. Next came John Fisher. Fisher was examined by Richard Rich under false pretenses on May 7, 1535, wherein Rich conveyed royal immunity to him for his honest response to the king's sincere request for his opinion on the issue of supremacy. Fisher imprudently complied and informed Rich that the king's claim was illicit. Shortly after having spoken with Rich, Fisher was indicted on June 9 for maliciously denying the king's supremacy. He was tried and convicted on June 17 and executed five days later on June 22. At trial, Fisher urged this defense: "The very statute that makes this speaking against the king's supremacy treason is only and precisely limited where such speech is spoken maliciously. And now all ye, my lords, perceive plainly that in my touching this claim of supremacy in the Church of England, in such sort as I did, as ye have heard, there was no manner of malice in me at all, and so I committed no treason."[204]

In another address to the judges, he honed in on the lack of malice: "I pray you my lords, consider that by all equity, justice, worldly honesty and courteous dealing, I cannot as the case stands, be directly charged therewith as with treason, though I had spoken the words in deed the same being not spoken maliciously, but in the way of advice and counsel, when it was requested of me by the king himself. And that favor the very words of the statute do give me, being made only against such as shall maliciously gainsay the king's supremacy, and none other."[205]

But the judges would hear none of it. An early biographer writes:

> To this it was answered to the bishop by some of the judges, utterly devoid of worldly shame, and affirmed by some of the residue, both that the word "maliciously" in the statute was of none effect, for that

none could speak against the king's supremacy by any manner or means but that the speaking against it was treason; and also that that message or promise to him from the king himself neither could nor did, by rigor of our law, in any wise discharge him; but that in so declaring his mind and conscience against the king's supremacy, though it were even at the king's own commandment and request, he by the statute committed treason.[206]

This is legal sophistry. Fisher's conviction made it two for two on the misapplication of the Act of Treason.

But the Carthusian monks and John Fisher were merely trial prep for the real prize. Like the case against John Fisher, the case against Thomas More was a one-witness case, Richard Rich being the witness. Unlike Fisher, More, the lawyer, had never been seduced by Rich's conniving assurances that the king only wanted his honest opinion of the supremacy. If that were so, More knew the king already had his counsel on the issue. But that counsel had been given prior to the passage of the Act of Treason in November of 1534. The crown needed a post-act denial. And Richard Rich was just the man for the job.

Rich testified to his version of a conversation he had with More in the Tower on June 12 in the presence of two other men, Sir Richard Southwell and Master Palmer. The conversation dealt with "the putting of cases" in hypothetical form. The thrust of Rich's testimony was that More denied Parliament had the authority to make the king Supreme Head of the Church of England. It was a brazen lie, uncorroborated by Southwell or Palmer. More upbraided Rich in the sharpest of terms, as we read earlier, telling him that he was sorrier for Rich's perjury than for his own peril.

More denied the making of the inculpatory statement. He pointed out the logical inconsistency of maintaining silence on the subject for over a year and suffering the resulting indignities and pains of imprisonment only to reveal his mind to Rich, someone he and others knew to be untrustworthy. But ever the lawyer, he said that even if he did reveal his mind in the "putting of cases" one to another, it was not malicious:

> And if I had done so indeed, my lords, as Master Rich has sworn seeing it was spoken but in familiar secret talk, nothing affirming, and only in putting of cases, without other displeasant circumstances, it cannot justly be taken to be spoken maliciously; and where there is no malice, there can be no offense. And over this I can never think, my lords, that so many worthy bishops, so many honorable peronsages, and many other worshipful, virtuous, wise and well learned men, as at the making of the law were in the parliament assembled, ever meant to have any man punished by death in whom there could be found no malice, taking malitia for maleveolentia; for if malita be generally taken for sin, no man is there then than can excuse himself.[207]

He then brilliantly and irrefutably analogized the language of the treason statute to that of the more common statutory crime of forcible entry: "And only this word maliciously is in the statute material, as this term forcibly is in the statute of forcible entries, by which statute if a man enters peaceably, and put not his adversary out forcibly, it is no offense, but if he put him out forcibly, then by that statute it is an offense, and so be punished by this term forcibly."[208]

The adverb *maliciously* has the same effect as the adjective *forcible*. Notwithstanding this powerful argument of law, the judges submitted the case to the jury on the perjurious testimony of a single uncorroborated witness concerning a conversation about hypothetical cases. The jury took fifteen minutes to find More guilty.

There are surviving descriptions of the trial by eyewitnesses. They are contained in a curious report by one Reginald Pole, a cousin to King Henry VIII and the eventual cardinal archbishop of Westminster. Pole compiled the statements of witnesses in a report he delivered to King Henry VIII on May 27, 1536, after he was safely away from England and beyond the king's reach. In that report, Pole quotes witnesses who heard More's passionate defense based upon the rule of law. The prosecution argued that More's silence was malignant, a "sign of an evil mind" and thus treasonous. More would have none of it. He argued that the Act of Treason had been passed after he had been sentenced to perpetual prison for not taking the oath following the Act of Succession. He was thus legally dead and not subject to the subsequent Act of Treason. But even if so, he had said nothing to anybody about the supremacy, contenting himself from that day forward with a contemplation of Christ's passion, and paying no attention to parliamentary legislation. At law, he argued, his silence implied consent so that if anything, the facts showed support, not denial, of the king's title.

Pole reports the judges' response as follows: "This word was received in such a way by the other seated judges that they believed that this judicial process which seemed almost to have collapsed could be reconstituted by this word [malice] alone. Even though no one had any charge to make they nevertheless all cried out together 'Malice, malice.' They proposed no deed or speech as proof of malice, but only silence. And in this way once again, like a wild beast almost escaped from the snares, the innocent man seemed trapped in the accusation."[209]

And trapped he was: "But now the twelve men, who according to the custom of our country have the power of life and death in trials, were called forward. And these men, since they had the word 'Malice,' which had sounded throughout the whole courtroom fixed in their ears and minds, made no delay—in fact it was a wonder that they could so quickly come to agreement. They immediately made their pronouncement in English, 'Guilty.'"

The More trial jury like the intimidated Carthusian jury had taken their cue.

Pole's account claims to be derived from eyewitnesses. It is consistent in parts with other accounts, the memoirs of one of the judges, Judge Spellman, and with a contemporaneous account in a French newspaper (for who could publish in England?). But its emphasis and accusatory purpose is unique. Pole's purpose was to chastise a king who had lost his way. He wrote, "For a moment, however, let us explain the form of that renowned trial in which More was condemned, so that one might better understand who it was who presided over that trial—Satan." [210]And in describing the extraordinary utterances of the judges, "malice, malice," he likened it to a different trial in a different day when the multitude cried out, "Crucify him. Crucify him."

The convictions strike at the hearts of lawyers who seek after justice and are concerned with due process. They reflect the total corruption of the legal process by ambitious, sycophantic, corrupt men, with deadly consequences to holy men. They remind one that perfect justice does not hold sway on earth and that our justice system is only as good as the men and women who administer it. More said, "If we lived in a State where virtue was profitable, common sense would make us good, and greed would make us saintly. And we'd live like animals or angels in the happy land that needs no heroes. But since in fact we see that avarice, anger, envy, pride, sloth, lust and stupidity commonly profit far beyond humility, charity, fortitude, justice and thought, and have to choose to be human at all . . . why then perhaps we must stand fast for a little—even at the risk of being heroes."[211]

Thankfully for our unhappy time and for those who seek to stand fast, we have the heroic examples of John Fisher and Thomas More.

CHAPTER 12

Condemned

"I die the King's good servant, and God's first."

As we saw at the conclusion of our last chapter, Reginald Pole was prompted by the judicial incantation of "malice, malice" to think of a distant trial where a just man was condemned to death for claiming a spiritual kingship beyond the realm of earthly potentates. In that distant time, like in the sixteenth century, and even today, those in power tend to exert their secular will, squeezing the spiritual life out of the citizen. One of the lessons flowing from the lives of Fisher and More is that the pursuit of truth is a costly thing. It costs energy to study and come to an understanding of the truth. One is then challenged to pursue the truth, which is often costly in terms of loss of position, human respect, and potentially one's life.

Those in power insist that people of faith ignore the truth. The coercion, subtle at first, grows in intensity, demanding that one conform and acquiesce to power. Fisher and More felt that demand and bent to it to the extent possible. Fisher was willing to swear to an oath subject to the limitation *quantum per legem Dei licet* ("as far as the law of God permits").

More was willing to resign the lord chancellorship and retire to Chelsea. But pushed too far, they would bend no more. And here we find them, first imprisoned, then interrogated, tried, and now subject to condemnation.

They suffered much and lost everything. But their spirits were strong, and their essence was revealed in these last days. More's response to interrogation sets the scene: "My whole study shall be on the passion of Christ. I do nobody harm. I say no harm. I think none harm, but wish everybody good. And if that be not enough to keep a man alive, in good faith I long not to live."[212]

After the pronouncement of guilt, Fisher said, "Truly my Lords, if that which I have before spoken be not sufficient, I have no more to say but only to desire Almighty God to forgive them that have condemned me for I think they know not what they have done."[213]

As he was marched back to the Tower, he thanked the guards who attended to him. In doing so, he displayed this magnanimity:

> "I thank you masters all, for the pains ye have taken this day in going and coming from hence to Westminister and hither again." And this spoke he with so lusty a courage and so amiable a countenance and his color so well come to him as though he had come from a great and honorable feast. And his gesture and his behavior showed such a certain inward gladness in his heart that any man might easily see that he joyously longed and looked for the bliss and joys of heaven, and

that he inwardly rejoiced that he was so near unto his death for Christ's cause.[214]

More was equally magnanimous. To the judges who pronounced the sentence, he said:

> More have I not to say, my Lords, but that like as the blessed Apostle St. Paul, as we read in the Acts of the Apostles, was present and consented to the death of St. Stephen, and kept their clothes that stoned him to death, and yet be they now both holy Saints in heaven, and shall continue there friends for ever, so I sincerely trust, and thereafter heartily pray, that though your Lordships have now here on the earth been Judges to my condemnation, we may yet hereafter in heaven merrily all meet together to our everlasting salvation, and thus I desire Almighty God to preserve and defend the King's Majesty and to send him good counsel.[215]

Vision and mission come together. Vision of a heaven more wonderful than imaginable and a mission of fidelity to God. In the Tower, More annotates the top of his prayer book with the thought "to think my greatest enemies my best friends;" at the bottom of the page, he scribbles "for the brethren of Joseph could never have done him so much good with their love and favor as they did with their malice and hatred."[216]

In this dark night of time, nothing seems to remain of the spiritual. Except the soul who sees beyond, who sees himself surrounded by a great cloud of witnesses, who throws off everything that hinders him, and finishes the race strong, eyes fixed elsewhere, on the author and perfecter of faith.

This is where we find our subjects when the trials are over, the verdicts read, and sentences pronounced. It is an awful sentence: "You are to be drawn on a hurdle through the city of London to Tyburn, there to be hanged till you be half dead, after that cut down yet alive, your bowels to be taken out of your body and burned before you, your privy parts cut off, your head cut off, your body divided in four parts, and your head and body to be set at such places as the King shall assign."[217]

"Mercifully," Henry commuted each sentence to beheading.

We all know More's response. G. K. Chesterton referred to More as "the man who died laughing," which resonates with then Pope John Paul II's description of him when he declared More the patron of statesmen and politicians: there was "harmony between the natural and supernatural" which enabled him to live "his intense public life with a simple humility marked by good humor even at the moment of his execution."[218]

More asked his executioner for help up the steps of the scaffold, telling him he would see his own way down. He warned him of his short neck and asked that he strike clean. He kissed the executioner and told him, "Thou will give me this day greater benefit than ever any mortal man can be able to give me." He recited Psalm 51, which begins, "Have mercy upon me, O God, according to thy lovingkindness."[219]

And of course, he uttered the famous line: "I die the King's good servant, and God's first." These words confirm More's unity of life. They also challenge the king. For in saying he dies the king's good servant and God's first, More echoes Henry's exhortation to him six years before in naming him lord chancellor of England: "First look to God and after God to [me]."[220] And so More did throughout his service to the king even as he mounted the steps of the scaffold. I doubt any sentence uttered by any person of that time is more remembered today.

But of the last day of John Fisher's life, little is known.

In the early morning hours of June 22, around 5:00 a.m., the Tower lieutenant came to Fisher with good news and bad news. The good news was that the king, in his mercy, had commuted his sentence from all that hanging, cutting, bowel removing, burning, and dividing to simple beheading. The bad news was that it was going to take place at 9:00 a.m., a mere four hours later. Fisher's reaction was to thank the guard and resume sleeping.[221] Fisher's life of virtue led him to respond to the news of his imminent execution by taking a nap!

At nine, he got up, dressed in his finest clothes, and told his servant that this was his marriage day and "it behooves us therefore to dress for the solemnity of that marriage."[222]

He then took a copy of the New Testament, crossed himself and went down to the courtyard to await the sheriffs. Much like Augustine did a millennia before,[223] Fisher opened the New Testament at random and began to read from the book of John 17:3–5: "And this is eternal life, that they know you, the only true God, and Jesus Christ whom you have sent. I glorified you on earth, having accomplished the work that you gave me to do. And now, Father, glorify me in your own presence with the glory that I had with you before the world existed."

He closed the book and remarked: "Here is learning enough for me even to my life's end."[224]

At the scaffold, he told the gathered people that he died for Christ's holy Catholic Church, asked God to save the king and the realm, and prayed "that he may hold his holy hand over it and send the king good counsel."[225]

He knelt and sang the *Te Deum*.[226] He then prayed Psalm 31, which reads in pertinent part:

> In thee, O Lord, do I put my trust. . . .
> I am forgotten as a dead man out of mind:
>   I am like a broken vessel.
> For I have heard the slander of many:
>   fear was on every side:
> while they took counsel together against me,
>   they devised to take away my life.
> But I trusted in thee, O Lord:
>   I said, Thou art my God.[227]

Then he stretched out his body. "The headsman struck one blow at the outstretched body, and the head of the first can- onized cardinal martyr, like the Baptist's head he had so long honored, had won its title to a place for ever on the altar of sacrifice."[228]

After he was beheaded, they stripped him and left him naked overnight, then threw him in a shallow grave the next morning. His head was "parboiled"[229] and set up on London Bridge. Two weeks later, it was taken down and thrown in the river to make room for the head of Thomas More.

A difficult place to end—two heads on a pole—when all along it has been my hope to present these men to you in an attractive way, as lives worthy of imitation. But maybe this is a good place to end. For when all is said and done, we stand where More stood when warned that the wrath of the king is death: "Is that all my lord? Then in good faith, there is no more difference between your grace and me, but that I shall die today and you tomorrow."[230] "For a man may lose his head and have no harm."[231]

And that is a message for all seasons.

Appendix

This appendix provides material should the reader wish to imitate in a small way the approach of John Fisher or Thomas More. It is inspired by an event which occurred more than forty years ago in my life. Then, I was a law student attending a seminar on ethics and politics, which focused on, among other things, a nineteenth-century member of Parliament, William Wilberforce. Wilberforce advocated political reform in England, inspired in part by the Great Awakening associated with John Wesley, and led a successful reform movement against the slave trade in England and a general reform of culture. He was part of a group of evangelical Christians known as "the Clapham Sect," named after the London suburb of Clapham where they all lived. These men, much like the Christian Humanists of the sixteenth century of which More was a member, communed for Bible study, prayer, and fellowship, and encouraged each other in their respective vocations.

The law professor giving the seminar rejected the evangelical faith of the members of the Clapham Sect. Yet he was fascinated by their effective communal action. He undertook a thirty-day experiment in which he tried to live as they had lived. If they prayed in the morning, he prayed in the morning. If they attended Bible study at night, he did the same. If they worshipped on Sunday, he put on his best on the first of the week and went to church. He concluded that during the thirty-day period, he experienced a greater sense of contentment, fulfillment, and love for his fellow man. He insisted he was not proselytizing our class, for at the end of thirty days, he remained as he was. He sensed, however, that he was calmer and more peaceful as a result of imitating the group in question.

He recommended the experiment in the same spirit that I am offering this appendix. Use the prayers, devotions, and reading as you see fit: perhaps a nine-day novena; a penitential psalm or a Fisher meditation for every day of the week; a reflection on the qualities of St. Thomas More set forth in Pope St. John Paul II's *Moto Propio*; and perhaps ending a day with the Te Deum. If you are a lawyer, the prayer attributed to St. Thomas More is outstanding, and whether lawyer or layman, so is the Prayer for Detachment from More's notations in his Prayer Book compiled by the Center for Thomas More Studies. Or do any combination of the above. Perhaps the spiritual, emotional, and intellectual excellence pursued by these special friends of God may manifest itself to you in similar fashion as described by that law professor decades ago.

Novena to Saints Thomas More and John Fisher

Nihil Obstat: Reverend Matthew Kauth, STD
           February 19, 2021

A "novena" (Latin for "nine") of prayer is a nine-day period of private or public prayer for a specific petition. It is modeled after the example given by our Lord to the Apostles. Having exhorted them to accomplish the Great Commission, he instructed them to return to Jerusalem after his ascension and to await the coming of the Holy Spirit (Acts 1:12, 14). After nine days, during which they devoted themselves to prayer, the Holy Spirit came upon them at Pentecost.

Elements of this pattern of nine days of petition and prayer include a mental state of confidence and perseverance—important qualities of efficacious prayer. "Then Jesus told them a parable (about the persistent widow) to show them they should always pray and never give up" (Lk 18:1). And from Matthew's Gospel: "Ask and it will be given to you, seek and you will find, knock and the door will be opened to you" (Mt 7:7).

What follows is a novena to Saints John Fisher and Thomas More seeking their intercession on a particular matter, while meditating on their inspirational lives and contemplating relevant Scripture.

Day 1

1. Make sign of the Cross
2. Say the Act of Contrition
3. Meditation

Truth

Thomas More resigned his lofty office as lord chancellor rather than violate his conscience concerning the king's "great matter." John Fisher stood before the king at the legatine hearing and declared that he was a "professor of the truth; I know that God is truth itself, nor he never spoke but truth." Each man believed his eternal soul depended upon his speaking the truth.

Pope St. John Paul II's observation of Thomas More is equally true of John Fisher: "Precisely because of the witness which he bore, even at the price of his life, to the primacy of truth over power, Saint Thomas More is venerated as an imperishable example of moral integrity."

With More, we pray, "Give me the grace, good Lord, to set the world at naught; to set my mind upon thee . . . to walk the narrow way that leadeth to life."

4. Scripture

Lord Jesus, your Word tells us that you came from the Father "full of grace and truth," (Jn 1:14) and that you are "the way, and the truth, and the life" (Jn 14:6). Let us read these words, believe these words, live these words.

5. Petition

Dear Saints Thomas More and John Fisher, lovers of life, triumphant in death, I ask that you intercede for me, confident that you will advocate for me before God's throne with the same zeal and diligence that marked your careers on earth. If it be in accord with God's will, obtain for me the favor I seek, namely _____.

6. Concluding Prayers
    Our Father
    Hail Mary
    Glory Be

Day 2

1. Make sign of the Cross
2. Say the Act of Contrition
3. Meditation

Vanity

Thomas More reluctantly took employment in the king's court. He knew he had "no cause to be proud thereof, for if my head would win him a castle in France, it should not fail to go." John Fisher was not fooled by the extravagance of the king's "Field of the Cloth of Gold," later preaching: "Our eyes have seen many pleasures, many gay sights, many wonderful things that have appeared and seemed to us joyous and comfortable. But yet all these were but dull and dark images of the perfect comfort which the blessed saints have now above in the kingdom of heaven."

There exists no title, no castle on earth, no amount of gold to equal the faithful believer's heavenly reward.

4. Scripture

Lord Jesus, your Word tells us that we have been raised with Christ and should set are hearts on things above, where Christ is seated at the right hand of God, that we should set our "affections on things above, not on things of the earth" (Col 3:1–2). For "where your treasure is, there will your heart be also" (Mt 6:21).

5. Petition

Dear Saints Thomas More and John Fisher, lovers of life, triumphant in death, I ask that you intercede for me, confident that you will advocate for me before God's throne with the same zeal and diligence that marked your careers on earth. If it be in accord with God's will, obtain for me the favor I seek, namely _____.

6. Concluding Prayers
   Our Father
   Hail Mary
   Glory Be

Day 3

1. Make sign of the Cross
2. Say the Act of Contrition
3. Meditation

Heaven

Visited in the prison tower by his beloved daughter Meg, Thomas More gazes out the window and what does he see? Three Carthusian monks being led off to their execution because they would not compromise their faith at the insistence of the king. More tells her: "Do you not see Meg, that these blessed fathers are now as cheerfully going to their deaths as bridegrooms to their marriage?"

John Fisher awoke on the day of his execution, donned his best clothes, and said, "This is my marriage day."

These thoughts anticipate by three centuries that of St. John Henry Newman, who felt that a Christian should look forward to death with the joy schoolboys feel as they prepare for Christmas vacation.

May we have before us this vision of joy and celebration of the kingdom prepared for those who believe.

4. Scripture
Lord Jesus, your Word tells us not to fear those who kill the body but cannot kill the soul (Mt 10:28). For "no eye has seen, no ear has heard, no mind has conceived what God has prepared for those who love him" (1 Cor 2:9; quoting Is 64:4).

5. Petition
Dear Saints Thomas More and John Fisher, lovers of life, triumphant in death, I ask that you intercede for me, confident that you will advocate for me before God's throne with the same zeal and diligence that marked your careers on earth. If it be in accord with God's will, obtain for me the favor I seek, namely _____.

6. Concluding Prayers
   Our Father
   Hail Mary
   Glory Be

Day 4

1. Make sign of the Cross
2. Say the Act of Contrition

3. Meditation

Detachment

When informed his house was broken into and goods stolen, St. John Fisher said, "Is that all? Then let us go to dinner and be merry and thank God for all that we have still remaining and look better to it than we did to the rest before."

Similarly, when Thomas More was informed that his manor at Chelsea had partially burned and all his barns were destroyed, he wrote his wife Alice: "I pray you and my children and your household be merry in God." For thus he perceived the fire to be an act of divine providence to teach the family the insignificance of material goods. Everyone, he said, "should go to church and give thanks."

Material goods given by a gracious God are meant to edify and not to enslave. May we experience the freedom that comes from detachment from the things of earth, and attachment to the things of God.

4. Scripture

Lord Jesus, your Word tells us to be mindful of the seed sown in thorns where "the cares of this world, and the deceitfulness of riches, and the desire for other things come in and choke the word, making it unfruitful" (Mk 4:19). "But seek first the kingdom of God and his righteousness and all these things shall be added unto you" (Mt 6:33).

5. Petition

Dear Saints Thomas More and John Fisher, lovers of life, triumphant in death, I ask that you intercede for me, confident that you will advocate for me before God's throne with the same zeal and diligence that marked your careers on earth. If it be in accord with God's will, obtain for me the favor I seek, namely _____.

6. Concluding Prayers
   Our Father
   Hail Mary
   Glory Be

Day 5

1. Make sign of the Cross
2. Say the Act of Contrition
3. Meditation

Pursuit of Truth

Fisher wrote concerning the king's great matter that "he had taken great pains to arrive at the truth and he could not change his mind without injury to both his reputation and his conscience." More told his daughter Meg, "For the instruction of my conscience in the matter I have not slightly looked, but my many years studied and advisedly considered, and never could see or hear that thing, and I think I never shall, that could induce my own mind to think otherwise than I do."

Diligent study matters, but *what* we study matters most. Fisher uses the metaphor of a book for the study of Christ's saving work on the cross: "Thus whoever with a meek heart and a true faith muses and marvels over this most wonderful book (I speak of the Crucifix), he shall come to more fruitful knowledge than many others who each day study their common books. This book may suffice for the study of the true Christian man all the days of his life. In this book he may find all things that are necessary for the health of his soul."

May we have the discipline to study the truth, a desire to speak the truth and the courage to witness to the truth.

4. Scripture
Lord Jesus, your Word tells us that you are the way, and the truth, and the life, let us come to the Father through you (Jn 1:14). May we "speak of your statutes before kings" and "not be put to shame" (Ps 119:46).

5. Petition
Dear Saints Thomas More and John Fisher, lovers of life, triumphant in death, I ask that you intercede for me, confident that you will advocate for me before God's Throne with the same zeal and diligence that marked your careers on earth. If it be in accord with God's will, obtain for me the favor I seek, namely _____.

6. Concluding Prayers:
Our Father
Hail Mary
Glory Be

Day 6:

1. Make sign of the Cross
2. Say the Act of Contrition
3. Meditation

Christ's Passion

Bishop Fisher's last surviving sermon refers to his constant theme, Christ on the Cross: "Is it not a wonderful thing, that he, that is the Lord and author of all liberty, would thus be bound with ropes and nailed hand and foot unto the Cross?"

More, like Fisher, turns to a contemplation of the passion of Christ when confined in the Tower: "If we could and would with due compassion conceive in our minds a right imagination and remembrance of Christ's bitter painful Passion—of the many sore bloody strokes that the cruel tormentors gave Him with rods and whips upon every part of His holy tender body; of the scornful crown of sharp thorns beaten down upon His holy head, so strait and so deep that on every part His blessed blood issued out and streamed down; of His lovely limbs drawn and stretched out upon the cross, to the intolerable pain of His sore-beaten veins and sinews, feeling anew, with the cruel stretching and straining, pain far surpassing any cramp in every part of His blessed body at once; of the great long nails then cruelly driven with the hammer through His holy hands and feet; of His body, in this horrible pain, lifted up and let hang, with all its weight bearing down upon the painful wounded places so grievously pierced with nails; and in such torment

without pity, but not without much scorn, suffered to be
pined and pained the space of more than three long hours,
till He Himself gave over His spirit; after which yet, to show
the mightiness of their malice, after His holy soul departed,
they pierced His holy heart with a sharp spear, at which
issued out the holy blood and water, whence His holy sacraments have inestimable secret strength—if we could, I say,
remember these things, in such a way as would God that we
would, I verily suppose that the consideration of His incomparable kindness could not fail so to inflame our key-cold
hearts, and set them on fire with His love, that we should
find ourselves not only content but also glad and desirous to
suffer death for His sake who so marvelous lovingly forbore
not to sustain so far passing death for ours."

May we, in our freedom, contemplate our Savior's willingness to be bound in love to the cross.

4. Scripture
Lord Jesus, your Word tells us that for the joy set before
him, Christ endured the cross (Hb 12:2). He suffered for us,
leaving us an example, that we should "follow in his steps"
(1 Pt 2:21).

5. Petition
Dear Saints Thomas More and John Fisher, lovers of life, triumphant in death, I ask that you intercede for me, confident
that you will advocate for me before God's Throne with the
same zeal and diligence that marked your careers on earth.
If it be in accord with God's will, obtain for me the favor I
seek, namely _____.

6. Concluding Prayers:
Our Father
Hail Mary
Glory Be

Day 7

1. Make sign of the Cross
2. Say the Act of Contrition
3. Meditation

Fortitude

When threatened by the king's henchmen with imprisonment, confiscation of property, and even death, More responds that "these terrors be arguments for children not for me." More knew that one can "lose his head but have no harm."

Fisher faces down the king before the legatine counsel, "No sir, not I," denying that he ever signed an affidavit in support of the king's divorce. Knowing that the "wrath of kings is death," he refuses to yield to power.

As a result of their courageous stands, both men were stripped of all that mattered to them on earth, yet they stood fast for the cause of Christ. In life, and with their lives, they declare with Job: "The Lord gives and the Lord takes away. Blessed be the name of the Lord" (1:21).

4. Scripture
Lord Jesus, your Word tells us too many times to count to not be afraid. You said to your disciples, "Be not afraid of

them that kill the body, and after that have no more that they can do" (Lk 12:4).

5. Petition

Dear Saints Thomas More and John Fisher, lovers of life, triumphant in death, I ask that you intercede for me, confident that you will advocate for me before God's Throne with the same zeal and diligence that marked your careers on earth. If it be in accord with God's will, obtain for me the favor I seek, namely _____.

6. Concluding Prayers
    Our Father
    Hail Mary
    Glory Be

Day 8

1. Make sign of the Cross
2. Say the Act of Contrition
3. Meditation

Love

In Bishop Fisher's meditation *The Way to Perfect Religion*, written from a Tower cell for the benefit of his sister, he describes love as the principal thing that makes any work easy, even if the "the work be right painful of itself." Without love, no labor can be comfortable to the doer. In fact, "great fervor and love to the service of God" makes life "a very paradise and heavenly joy in this world."

In the Tower, More writes a prayer, probably using coal after the guards removed his writing instruments: "To think my greatest enemies my best friends; for the brethren of Joseph could never have done him so much good with their love and favor as they did with their malice and hatred."

Love of God and neighbor converts enemies, makes labor a joy, and gives meaning to life. May we, through the examples of your saints, live in love with you, and with each other.

4. Scripture

Lord Jesus, your Word commands us to love one another as you have loved us (Jn 15:12). It assures us that perfect love casts out all fear (1 Jn 4:18) and instructs us that greater love has no man than he lay down his life for another (Jn 15:13).

5. Petition

Dear Saints Thomas More and John Fisher, lovers of life, triumphant in death, I ask that you intercede for me, confident that you will advocate for me before God's Throne with the same zeal and diligence that marked your careers on earth. If it be in accord with God's will, obtain for me the favor I seek, namely _____.

6. Concluding Prayers:
   Our Father
   Hail Mary
   Glory Be

Day 9

1. Make sign of the Cross
2. Say the Act of Contrition
3. Meditation

Forgiveness

More and Fisher are sentenced to death. The mere reading of the sentence shocks our ears: "You are to be drawn on a hurdle through the city of London to Tyburn, there to be hanged till you be half dead, after that cut down yet alive, your bowels to be taken out of your body and burned before you, your privy parts cut off, your head cut off, your body divided in four parts, and your head and body to be set at such places as the King shall assign." "Mercifully," the king commuted the sentence to beheading.

More and Fisher meet it all with equanimity. To his lords who pronounced the sentence, More said, "So I sincerely trust, and thereafter heartily pray, that though your Lordships have now here in the earth been Judges to my condemnation, we may yet hereafter in heaven merrily all meet together to our everlasting salvation."

Fisher responded, "I have no more to say but only desire Almighty God to forgive them that have thus condemned me, for I think they know not what they have done." We, too, have opportunity to respond to evil with love and so to emulate these worthy servants of the Lord as they follow Him.

4. Scripture

Lord Jesus, your Word tells us to bless those who persecute us (Rom 12:14), to put away all malice, bitterness, wrath, anger, and slander, and to be kind to one another, tenderhearted, forgiving one another as God in Christ forgave us (Eph 4:31).

5. Petition

Dear Saints Thomas More and John Fisher, lovers of life, triumphant in death, I ask that you intercede for me, confident that you will advocate for me before God's Throne with the same zeal and diligence that marked your careers on earth. If it be in accord with God's will, obtain for me the favor I seek, namely _____.

6. Concluding Prayers
   Our Father
   Hail Mary
   Glory Be

More's Prayer on Detachment[232]

Tower of London, 1534–1535

> Give me Thy grace, good Lord:
> To set the world at naught;
> To set my mind fast upon Thee,
> And not to hang upon the blast of men's mouths;
> To be content to be solitary,
> Not to long for worldly company;

Little and little utterly to cast off the world,
And rid my mind of all the business thereof;
Not to long to hear of any worldly things,
But that the hearing of worldly fantasies may be to
    me displeasant;
Gladly to be thinking of God,
Piteously to call for His help;
To lean unto the comfort of God,
Busily to labor to love Him;
To know mine own vility and wretchedness,
To humble and meeken myself under the mighty
    hand of God;
To bewail my sins past,
For the purging of them patiently to suffer adversity;
Gladly to bear my purgatory here,
To be joyful of tribulations;
To walk the narrow way that leadeth to life,
To bear the cross with Christ;
To have the last thing in remembrance,
To have ever afore mine eye my death, that is ever at
    hand;
To make death no stranger to me,
To foresee and consider the everlasting fire of hell;
To pray for pardon before the judge come,
To have continually in mind the Passion that Christ
    suffered for me;
For His benefits incessantly to give Him thanks,
To buy the time again that I before have lost;
To abstain from vain confabulations,
To eschew light foolish mirth and gladness;

Recreations not necessary, to cut off,
Of worldly substance, friends, liberty, life and all,
to set the loss at right naught for the winning of
    Christ;
To think my most enemies my best friends,
For the brethren of Joseph could never have done
    him so much good
with their love and favor as they did him with their
    malice and hatred.
These minds are more to be desired of every man
    than all the treasure of all the princes
and kings, Christian and heathen, were it gathered
    and laid together all upon one heap.

Prayer of St Thomas More[233]

For lawyers

Lord, grant that I may be able in argument,
accurate in analysis,
strict in study,
candid with clients,
and honest with adversaries.
Sit with me at my desk
and listen with me to my client's complaints,
read with me in my library,
and stand beside me in court,
so that today I shall not,
in order to win a point,
lose my soul. Amen.

Seven Prayers of St. John Fisher

Bishop John Fisher wrote *The Way to Perfect Religion*, while in the Tower, as a meditation on the name of Jesus, for his step-sister, Elizabeth White, a Dominican nun. It concludes with seven sentences, each a prayer to be used on successive days of the week.

Sunday

O blessed Jesu, make me to love Thee entirely.

Monday

O blessed Jesu, I would please you, but without Thy help I cannot.

Tuesday

O blessed Jesu, let me deeply consider the greatness of Thy love towards me.

Wednesday

O blessed Jesu, give unto me grace heartily to thank Thee for Thy benefits.

Thursday

O blessed Jesu, give me good will to serve Thee and to suffer.

Friday

O sweet Jesu, give me a natural remembrance of Thy Passion.

Saturday

O sweet Jesu, possess my heart, hold and keep it only to Thee.

Resume of Thomas More

THOMAS MORE

Chelsea, England | Thomas_More@kingscourt.gov

Experience

Lord Chancellor of England	1529-1532
Chancellor of the Duchy, Lancaster, England	1525-1529
Appointed to King's Council (one of four members)	1526
High Steward for Universities of Oxford, Cambridge	1525
Speaker of the House of Commons	1523
Knight of the Shire (MP), Middlesex, England	1523-1525
Under-Treasurer of the Exchequer	1521-1523
Made a Knight; Ambassador to Bruges, Calais	1521
King's Secretary, Chief Diplomat, Personal Advisor	1517-1521
King's Diplomat to Holy Roman Emperor Charles V	1517
Master of Requests	1514
Privy Councilor	1514
Under-Sheriff, City of London	1510
Member, Parliament (from Great Yarmouth)	1504
(from London)	1510
Lawyer "called to the Bar"	1502
Page to John Morton,	
Archbishop of Canterbury & Lord Chancellor	1490-1492

Education

Lincoln's Inn (one of England's four legal societies)	1496
New Inn (Inn of Chancery)	1494-1496

Oxford University   1492-1494
St. Anthony School

Publications

TRANSLATIONS OF LUCIAN (MANY DATES 1506–1534)
THE LIFE OF PICO DELLA MIRANDOLA, (1510)
(TRANSLATION)
A Merry Jest (1516)
Utopia (1516)
Latin Poems (1518, 1520)
Letter to Brixius (1520)
Responsio ad Lutherum (1523)
A Dialogue Concerning Heresies (1529, 1530)
Supplication of Souls (1529)
Letter Against Frith (1532)
The Confutation of Tyndale's Answer (1532, 1533)
Apology (1533)
Debellation of Salem and Bizance (1533)
The Answer to a Poisoned Book (1533)
The History of King Richard III (c. 1513–1518)
The Four Last Things (c. 1522)
A Dialogue of Comfort Against Tribulation (1534)
Treatise Upon the Passion (1534)
Treatise on the Blessed Body (1535)
Instructions and Prayers (1535)
De Tristitia Christi (1535)

Personal Date of Birth: February 7, 1478
Marriage: Jane Colt (1505), Alice Middleton (1511)
Children: Margaret Roper, Elizabeth More, Cicely More, John More
                  Adopted Anne Cresacre More, Margaret Giggs Clement

INTERESTS: Latin & Greek, Home-Schooling, Musical Harmony, Rhetoric, Carthusian Monasticism

Resume of John Fisher

JOHN FISHER
Rochester, England | John_Fisher@cambridge.edu.com

Experience

Cardinal	1535
Counselor to Queen Catherine of Aragon	1532-1535
Founder, St John's College, Cambridge University	1516
Appointed, English Representative	
at the Fifth Council of Lateran	1512
Founder, Christ's College, Cambridge University	1506
Bishop of Rochester	1504-1535
Chancellor of Cambridge University	1504-1535
(re-elected annually for ten years then appointed for life)	
Vice-Chancellor of Cambridge University	1501-1504
President of Queen's College	1505-1508
Lady Margaret Professor of Divinity, Cambridge University	1505
Tutor, Confessor, Chaplain	
to Lady Margaret (mother of Henry VII)	1502
Proctor Cambridge University (Age 25)	1494
Vicar of Northallerton, Yorkshire	1491
Ordained as a Priest (despite being under canonical age)	1491
Elected Fellow Cambridge University	1491

Education

Cambridge University Masters	1491
Cambridge University, BA	1487
Beverly Grammar School	1477-1487

Publications

26 works, See Gillow's Bibliographical Dictionary of the English Catholics (London, s.d.), II, 262–270.

Personal Date of Birth: October 9, 1469
INTERESTS: Book Collector, humanist (promoter of the "New Learning"), theologian

Acknowledgments

My wife, Ann, is a very good artist. I have often watched in bemusement at her creative process. It seems she spends 10 percent of her time on 90 percent of a painting and 90 percent of her time on the last 10 percent. While the work of art remains in her possession, it is never quite finished, never perfect. As attributed to the French poet Valery, "A work of art is never finished, just abandoned." I understand this phenomenon better after working through this writing process. It seemed that there was always something more to learn about John Fisher and Thomas More—and a better way to communicate that knowledge. But at some point, I had to let go and submit this work for publication. But before I do, there are a few people I would like to acknowledge.

My knowledge of John Fisher and Thomas More is derived from reading about them. For the joy these books brought to me as well as for the factual underpinnings of this book, I express gratitude to the many authors listed in the bibliography, and especially to Gerard B. Wegemer, PhD, director of the Center for Thomas More Studies.

Although the information that went into this book was acquired through an adult lifetime of reading, the writing process largely occurred during 2020, the year of the COVID-19 pandemic. The normal stresses and challenges of life were exacerbated by the twenty-first-century equivalent of the sixteenth-century *hantavirus* which wreaked world-wide havoc. The silver lining for me was the cessation of travel, the reduced number of trials and hearings that usually comprise a judge's day, and the quietude and reflection that sometimes accompanied a largely quarantined society—when it wasn't going absolutely insane during an election year.

Greatly aiding the deliberative process was the generosity of family and friends who not only respected the need for concentration but also provided the creative space for the writing to occur. Especial thanks go to my daughter Meg—I mean Kim—and her husband, John, and to Cricket and Craig Stewart for allowing me access to their happy places on Lake Hyco and Hartwell, respectively.

No acknowledgment is possible without expressing gratitude to the good people at TAN Books for their constant encouragement. Brian Kennelly, my editor (and former basketball player under my tutelage as a youth coach), made sure I did the "little things" to make this book better. My good friend Bob Gallagher and former law clerk Conor Gallagher, successive publishers of TAN, were indefatigable in their support. Thank you for sometimes treating deadlines as guidelines, and sometimes not.

Hadley Arkes contributed an insightful Foreword, but he did more than that. He affirmed a cherished friendship, entering its fifth decade. Thank you.

I also want to thank my nephew Jeff Conrad for his thoughtful contributions to this final product.

To my wife, Ann, children and grandchildren, thank you for being my *raison d'etre*.

To my God, *Ad majorem Dei gloriam*.

This, the thirty-first day of October 2020, All Hallows' Eve, and the twentieth anniversary of St. John Paul II's pronouncement of St. Thomas More as patron of statesmen and politicians.

Notes

Introduction

1   Michael Macklem, *God Have Mercy: The Life of John Fisher or Rochester* (Ottawa: Oberon Press, 1969).

2   Gerard B. Wegemer, *A Portrait of Courage* (Princeton: Scepter Publishers, 1998), p. 128.

3   *Henry VIII*, 2.2.

4   ssential Works of Thomas More, p. 1381.

5   Robert Bolt, *A Man For All Seasons*, (introduction).

6   Erasmus, *Ecclesiastes*, dedicatory preface, 1535.

7   G. K. Chesterton, *The Fame of Blessed Thomas More* (London: Sheed & Ward, 1929), p. 63.

8   Fisher lived an austere life. His one extravagance was his library, the envy of scholars all over Europe, and this author too.

9   Maria Dowling, *Fisher of Men: a Life of John Fisher, 1469-1535,* (Great Britain: Macmillan Press Ltd. 1999), p. 66.

10   Although not hagiographic, the tone of this book is relentlessly positive, the result of the author's belief that these inspiring lives are worthy of emulation. Yet one might wonder why there is not a more critical assessment of the seemingly less wholesome qualities of these men? For example, some would question Thomas More's approach to love and marriage. He married twice apparently for reasons other than romantic love. His first wife was Joanna (sometimes referred to as Jane), a "trainable" teenage country girl, who died from "sweating sickness" (or influenza) after having birthed four babies in six years. He quickly married his second wife, Alice, within a month after Joanna's death. He seems opportunistic here, there are kids to raise. Alice is ridiculed by Erasmus, and later depicted by Robert Bolt, as possessing a somewhat foolish and unattractive personality calling into question More's motivation for a quick re-marriage. Yet others disagree. John Guy portrays Alice as "at ease with herself," one who took charge of the household "from the moment she arrived;" and whose step-kids and

grand-kids loved her "as if she were their natural mother;" her "worldly wisdom, forthright speech and practical efficiency were exactly what Thomas [More] needed." Even Erasmus, an evicted guest, had to admit that More ""full entirely loved her" (Guy, *A Daughter's Love*, pp. 41–45). A second serious complaint against More and Fisher is their treatment of "heretics" whom Catholics today would refer to as separated brethren. Here a defense of "presentism" could be raised. There was a mere eighteen years between Luther's posting of his ninety-five theses at Wittenburg and More's execution. Fifteen hundred years of united Catholic Christianity preceded it. Ecumenism was non-existent. Modern day notions of religious pluralism and tolerance were foreign to sixteenth-century thought. The English culture was threatened by a revolutionary spirit that prompted scorched earth responses to protect the unity of Christendom in a way that is hard to fathom today. And a case could be made that there were fewer persecutions and more humane treatment under More's chancellorship and Fisher's bishopric than others. Yet the making of that case is beyond this book's purpose. The author would beg the questioning reader's indulgence. Don't let what you consider to be the subjects' least attractive traits prevent you from gleaning lessons from their otherwise worthy lives. A third complaint against More is that he appears to have disfavored sports. I don't know how someone can be so wise without the benefit of analogy to sports. I guess I will have to get past that.

11 Mark 6:7.

12 Vincent McNabb, *St. John Fisher* (Mediatrix Press, 1936), p. 9. Vincent Nichols, *St John Fisher: Bishop and Theologian in Reformation and Controversy* (Stoke-On-Trent: Alive Publishing, 2011), p. 20.

Chapter 1: Conscience

13 Although, in this regard, he seems to ignore or be unaware of the Deuteronomic command to marry the childless widow of your brother (Deuteronomy 25:5).

14 Macklem, *God Have Mercy*, p.87.

15 For a riveting account of the hearing by a contemporary, George Cavendish, see Michael Macklem, *God Have Mercy: The Life of*

John Fisher of Rochester (Ottawa: Oberon Press, 1969).

16   Ibid., pp. 96–110.

17   Ibid., p. 100.

18   Ibid., p. 101.

19   Ibid.

20   Ibid., p. 102.

21   Ibid.

22   Ibid, p. 103.

23   Macklem, *God Have Mercy*, p. 109.

24   Ibid., p. 143.

25   In acknowledgment of Fisher's greatness, the Catholic Church
      marks his feast day, and that of the better-known Thomas More,
      on June 22, the date of Fisher's execution. It is believed that Henry
      VIII rushed the execution of Fisher to avoid its falling on the Bap-
      tist's feast day two days later, which Henry feared would trigger
      unwanted comparisons of Henry to Herod.
          The Anglican Church celebrates both men's feast day on July 6,
      the date of More's execution. Thomas More was executed on the
      day of the celebration of the translation of the body of St. Thomas
      Beckett to Trinity Chapel, Oxford. The story of Beckett's murder
      by associates of Henry II was a national legend. More took partic-
      ular comfort from the fact he would be executed on Beckett's day:
      "I cumber you Margaret much, but I would be sorry if it should be
      any longer than tomorrow, for it is St Thomas Eve . . . and there-
      fore tomorrow I long to go to God." E. E. Reynolds, *The Field is
      Won: The Life and Death of Saint Thomas More* (Milwaukee: The
      Bruce Publishing Company, 1968), p. 375.

26   Macklem, *God Have Mercy*, p. 102.

27   Gerard Manley Hopkins, *Hopkins Poetry and Prose* (Knopf, New
      York, 1995), *Peace,* p. 75: "O surely, reaving Peace, my Lord
      should leave in lieu/Some Good! And so he does leave Patience
      exquisite,/That plumes to peace thereafter."

Chapter 2: Truth

28   William Roper, *The Mirrour of Vertue in Worldly Greatness or the
      Life of Sir Thomas More* (San Francisco: Ignatius Press, 2002), pp.
      105–6.

29   "We may not look at our pleasures to go to heaven in featherbeds;

it is not the way, for our Lord Himself went thither with great pain, and by many tribulations, which was the path wherein He walked thither, and the servant may not look to be in better case than his Master." Roper, *The Mirrour of Vertue in Worldly Greatness or the Life of Sir Thomas More*, p. 28.

30   Bolt, *A Man for All Seasons*, p. vii.

31   Quote attributed to St. Vincent Lerins, fifth-century theologian writing after the Church Council of Ephesus.

32   This resonates with all that is known of Fisher. Later, when about to be imprisoned, he was asked by administrators at St. John's College, which he founded, to sign off on documents related to amendments to the governing statutes of the college: "God's will be done," he said, "for I will never allow under my seal that thing which I have not well and substantially viewed and considered." Vincent McNabb, *St. John Fisher* (Mediatrix Press, 1936), p. 76.

33   Macklem, *God Have Mercy*, pp. 63–64.

34   John Henry Newman, *Certain Difficulties Felt By Anglicans in Catholic Teachings* (Longmans, Green, and Co., New York, 1892), pp. 171–347.

35   Ibid., p. 246.

36   Papal visit to Columbia, SC, on September 11, 1987 as part of an ecumenical conference on the campus of the University of South Carolina at Williams-Brice Stadium.

37   "Let justice be done though the heavens may fall." *Somerset v Stewart*, 98 ER 499 (1772).

38   Roper, *The Mirrour of Vertue in Worldly Greatness or the Life of Sir Thomas More*, p. 121.

39   Macklem, p. 76.

40   Roper, *Life*, p. 120.

41   Bolt, *A Man for All Seasons*, p. 132. This appears to be a license taken by Bolt. Bolt's play, *A Man for All Seasons*, is sometimes quoted herein even though it is subject to legitimate criticism by historian John Guy and others that it is "sumptuous drama but appalling history." Bolt not infrequently used a More communication—usually his letters to Meg—and turned it into dialogue, often beautiful dialogue, that captured the essence of a Morian thought. For instance, here, the actual incident involves a story More told his daughter Meg. In the story, a juror named "Company" is asked to side with the eleven other jurors against his conscience. He tells them, "I went over once for good company with

you, which is the cause I go now to hell, play you the good fellows now again with me, as I went for good company with you, so some of you go now for good company with me." Roper, pp. 132–33. What a prophetic utterance concerning the lack of courage that the Henrician juries would soon demonstrate in the treason trials soon to come of the Carthusian monks, John Fisher, and Thomas More.

[42]   Roper, *The Mirrour of Vertue in Worldly Greatness or the Life of Sir Thomas More*, p. 143.

[43]   acklem, *God Have Mercy*, p. 64.

[44]   eter Ackroyd, *The Life of Thomas More* (New York: Doubleday, 1998), p. 374.

[45]   Ibid., p. 397.

[46]   Ibid.

Chapter 3: Oath

[47]   North Carolina General Statutes (NCGS) Chapter 11 Section 11-1.

[48]   NCGS 11-2.

[49]   NCGS 11-3.

[50]   Guy, *A Daughter's Love*, p. 264.

[51]   Bolt, *A Man For All Seasons*, p. 132. This appears to be a license taken by Bolt. The actual incident involves his wife Alice telling him that "God regardeth the heart rather than the tongue and that the meaning of the oath thereby goeth upon that they think, and not upon that they say." Ackroyd, *The Life of Thomas More*, p. 361.

[52]   Rudyard Kipling, *Rewards and Fairies* (1910); The full poem is as follows

IF

If you can keep your head when all about you
    Are losing theirs and blaming it on you,
If you can trust yourself when all men doubt you,
    But make allowance for their doubting too;
If you can wait and not be tired by waiting,
    Or being lied about, don't deal in lies,
Or being hated, don't give way to hating,
    And yet don't look too good, nor talk too wise:

If you can dream—and not make dreams your master;
   If you can think—and not make thoughts your aim;
If you can meet with Triumph and Disaster
   And treat those two impostors just the same;
If you can bear to hear the truth you've spoken
   Twisted by knaves to make a trap for fools,
Or watch the things you gave your life to, broken,
   And stoop and build 'em up with worn-out tools:

If you can make one heap of all your winnings
   And risk it on one turn of pitch-and-toss,
And lose, and start again at your beginnings
   And never breathe a word about your loss;
If you can force your heart and nerve and sinew
   To serve your turn long after they are gone,
And so hold on when there is nothing in you
   Except the Will which says to them: 'Hold on!'

If you can talk with crowds and keep your virtue,
   Or walk with Kings—nor lose the common touch,
If neither foes nor loving friends can hurt you,
   If all men count with you, but none too much;
If you can fill the unforgiving minute
   With sixty seconds' worth of distance run,
Yours is the Earth and everything that's in it,
   And—which is more—you'll be a Man, my son!

53   John Guy, *A Daughter's Love, Thomas More & His Dearest Meg* (Houghton Mifflin Harcourt 2009), p. 33.

54   Roper, *The Mirrour of Vertue in Worldly Greatness or the Life of Sir Thomas* More, pp. 43–45.

Chapter 4: Vocation

55   John Henry Newman, *Apologia Pro Vita Sua*, pp. 239–40.

56   See the appendix for a modern iteration of what their resumes might look like.

57   Bolt, *A Man for All Seasons,* p. xxiii.

58   E. E. Reynolds, *The Field is Won,* p. 221.

59   More, *History of Richard III.*

60 John Fisher, *Exposition of the Seven Penitential Psalms* (Ignatius Press 1998), pp. 151–52.

61 Roper, *Life of Thomas More*, p. 66.

62 Basset, *Born for Friendship*, p. 105.

63 John Guy, *A Daughter's Love, Thomas More & His Dearest Meg* (Houghton Mifflin Harcourt, 2009), p. 162.

64 Ackroyd, The *Life of Thomas More*, p. 287.

65 Except for some revisionist historians who have recently attempted to redeem his reputation and in a certain sense impugn More's, see e.g. Hillary Mantel's *Wolf Hall* and *Bring Up the Bodies;* Diarmaid MacCulloch, *Thomas Cromwell* (New York: Viking, 2018).

66 Hilaire Belloc, *Characters of the Reformation* (San Francisco: Ignatius Press), p. 50.

67 Peter Ackroyd, *The History of England from Henry VIII to Elizabeth* (New York: Thomas Dunne Books, 2012), p. 150.

68 Bolt, *A Man For All Seasons*, p. 158.

69 English writer, poet, and Protestant martyr in 1546; one of two women tortured in the tower and burned at the stake.

70 The eldest surviving brother of Queen Jane Seymour, the third wife of King Henry VIII. He was lord protector of England from 1547 to 1549 during the minority of his nephew King Edward VI, but executed for treason in 1552.

71 Lady Jane Grey known as the "Nine Days Queen," the great-niece of Henry VII, who took the crown from Queen Mary I. A tragic figure used as a pawn in a political game, she was only seventeen when she was beheaded.

72 An English general and politician who led the government of the young King Edward VI from 1550 until 1553. He unsuccessfully tried to install Lady Jane Grey on the English throne after the King's death; executed in 1553.

73 Christopher Hollis, *Thomas More* (The Bruce Publishing Company, 1934), pp. 233–34.

74 Thomas More, *The Complete Works of St. Thomas More, Volume II, The History of King Richard III* (New Haven: Yale University Press, 1963).

75 "The world is a stage that's topsy turvy now. Everyman must play his part – or exit." Erasmus, *A Dialogue Between Antronius, a Voluptous Abbot, and Magdala, a Learned Woman.*

76 Heather Y. Wheeler, "Tudor Executions 1485–1603," Totally Timelines, September 28, 2019, https://www.totallytimelines.

com/tudor-executions-1485-1603/#:~:text=It%20is%20esti-mated%20that%20around,reigns%20of%20the%20Tudor%20Monarchs.

77   Macbeth 5:5, lines 17–28.

78   Roper, *The Mirrour of Vertue in Worldly Greatness or the Life of Sir Thomas More*, p. 46.

79   Gerard B. Wegemer, *A Portrait of Courage* (Princeton: Scepter Publishers, 1998), p. 181; citing *The Correspondence of Sir Thomas More*, p. 531–32.

80   Peter Ackroyd, *The Life of Thomas More*, p. 366.

81   Bernard Basset, *Born for Friendship*, p. 182.

82   Bolt, *A Man For All Seasons*, p. 162.

83   Christopher Hollis, *Thomas More* (The Bruce Publishing Company, 1934), pp. 229–30.

Chapter 5: Virus

84   John Guy, *A Daughter's Love*, pp. 37–38.

85   William Shakespeare (and others), *Sir Thomas More*, edited by Gerard B. Wegemer, CTMS Publication at the University of Dallas, 2020, Act 1, Scene 1, lines 78-90.

86   Ibid.

87   Ibid.

88   Reynolds, *The Field is Won*, p. 122; citing Hally, *Henry VIII*, ed. C. Whitley (1959), vol. 1, p. 159.

89   Ibid.

90   Reynolds, *Margaret Roper*, p. 56.

91   Ibid.

92   Ibid., pp. 12324.

93   Wegemer, *A Portrait of Courage*, p. 181.

94   Roper, *The Mirrour of Vertue in Worldly Greatness or the Life of Sir Thomas More*, p. 53.

95   Hollis, *Thomas More*, pp. 241–42.

96   Ibid., p. 237.

97   Wegemer, *A Portrait of Courage*, p. 220.

98   Ibid., p. 222.

Chapter 6: Family

99   Macklem, *God Have Mercy*, p. 11.

100   Ibid., p. 12.

101   Ibid., p. 12

102   Ibid., p. 54.

103   Nichols, *St. John Fisher*, p. 20.

104   Reynolds, *St. John Fisher*, p. 183

105   Hollis, *Thomas More*, p. 237.

106   Reynolds, *Saint John Fisher*, pp. 249–50.

107   Sayers died September 23, 2020.

108   Some who might not have grown up watching Gale Sayers every Sunday in the fall might know about him from the movie *Brian's Song* about the relationship between Brian Piccolo and Gale Sayers.

109   Psalms 6, 32, 38, 51, 102, 130, 143.

110   Psalm 129.

Out of the depths I have cried unto Thee, O Lord; Lord, hear my voice.

Let Thine ears be attentive to the voice of my supplication.

If Thou, O Lord, shalt mark our iniquities: O Lord, who can abide it?

For with Thee there is mercy: and by reason of Thy law I have waited on Thee, O Lord.

My soul hath waited on His word: my soul hath hoped in the Lord.

From the morning watch even unto night: let Israel hope in the Lord.

For with the Lord there is mercy: and with Him is plenteous redemption.

And He shall redeem Israel from all his iniquities.

111   Reynolds, *Margaret Roper*, p. 47.

112   Ibid., p. 18.

113   Ibid., p. 60.

114   On one occasion, Erasmus had attributed a letter to St. Cyprian when in fact, as Margaret discovered, it was written by Novatian, "a heretic."

115   *The Treatise of the Pater Noster*, a translation with additions of Erasmus's Greek work of the same name.

116   Guy, *A Daughters Love*, p. 62.

117 Wegemer, *A Portrait of Courage*, p. 80; citing *Selected Letters of St. Thomas More*, p. 105.

118 Ibid.

119 Sargent, Daniel, *Thomas More* (London, 1938), p.79.

120 Wegemer, *A Portrait in Courage*, p. 80.

121 Guy, *A Daughter's Love*, p. 239.

122 Ibid.

123 Ibid., p. 247–50.

124 Ibid., p. 235.

125 Roper, *Life*, p. 173.

126 Ibid., p. 149.

127 Guy, *A Daughter's Love*, p. 249.

128 Ibid.

129 Luke 2:29.

130 Kelly, Karlin, Wegemer, *Thomas More's Trial by Jury* (The Boydell Press, 2011), p. 194.

131 Guy, *A Daughter's Love*, pp. 262–63.

132 Roper, *The Mirrour of Vertue in Worldly Greatness or the Life of Sir Thomas More*, p. 176.

Chapter 7: Friendship

133 "Erasmus Letter to Ulrich von Hutton, July 23, 1519," accessed February 19, 2021, https://thomasmorestudies.org/wp-content/uploads/2020/09/EE999_OCR.pdf.

134 Campbell, *Erasmus Tyndale and more*, p. 19.

135 Ibid., p. 16.

136 Basset, *Born for Friendship*, p. 134.

137 Guy, *A Daughter's Love*, p. 82.

138 Campbell, Erasmus, Tyndale & More, p. 22.

139 Ibid., p. 22–23.

140 Ibid., p. 17–18; quoting G. V. Jourdan, *A History of the English Church in the Sixteenth Century*, p. xxx.

141 Macklem, *God Have Mercy*, p. 64.

142 Bridgett, *Life of Fisher*, p. 297.

143 C. S. Lewis, *The Weight of Glory*, p 45–46.

144 Basset, *Born for Friendship*, p. 161.

145 Ibid., p. 179.

146 Roper, *Life of Sir Thomas More*, p. 134.

147   Ibid., p. 120.

148   Ibid., p. 154.

149   Ibid., p. 65.

150   Ibid., p. 87–88.

151   Ibid., p. 99.

152   See, for example, Federal Rule of Evidence 804(2), Statement Under the Belief of Imminent Death (a statement about the cause or circumstance of death by a declarant while believing declarant's death to be imminent is an exception to the hearsay rule).

153   Wegemer, *A Portrait of Courage*, p. 192.

Chapter 8: Baptist

154   John Beverly was an eighth-century Benedictine bishop of York, England who was named John by Archbishop Theodore of Canterbury. St. John Beverly was a renowned preacher. His pastoral care anticipates that of his namesake Fisher as "he was diligent in visitation, considerate towards the poor, and exceedingly attentive to the training of students whom he maintained under his personal charge." Among other fascinating things, he ordained St. Bede. *Catholic Encyclopedia*, s.v. "Beverly, John."

155   June 24, two days after the date of the execution of John Fisher.

156   Macklem, *God Have Mercy*, p. 32.

157   Eds. Brendan Bradshaw and Eamon Duffy, *Humanism, Reform and the Reformation: The Career of Bishop John Fisher Cambridge* (Cambridge University Press, 1989), p. 103. Some referred to him as the greatest preacher living in England.

158   He did this in the misguided hope of inducing Henry to ease Fisher's custodial treatment. It had the reverse effect. He would be executed the next month, with Henry stating, "Well, let the Pope send him a hat when he will, but I will so provide that whensoever it commeth, he shall wear it on his shoulders for head he shall have none to set it on." Reynolds, *Saint John Fisher*, p. 264.

159   Skulls were in fact a devotional artifact lingering from medieval Catholicism.

160   Eds. Brendan Bradshaw and Eamon Duffy, *Humanism, Reform and the Reformation*, p. 218.

161   Ibid., p. 219

162   Ibid., quoted in T. E. Bridget, *Life of Fisher*, p. 170.

163   Mark 6:20.
164   Mark 6:14.
165   Shakespeare, *History of Henry VIII*, Act II, Scene 2.
166   Daniel-Rops, *The Protestant Reformation*, p. 469.
167   Mark 6:26.
168   Mark 6:21–27.
169   Daniel-Rops, *The Protestant Reformation*, p. 473.
170   Macklem, *God Have Mercy*, p. 76.

Chapter 9: Detachment

171   Roper, *The Mirrour of Vertue in Worldly Greatness or the Life of Sir Thomas More*, p. 22.
172   E. E. Reynolds, *Saint John Fisher* (New York: P.J. Kenedy & Sons), p. 81.
173   Ibid., p. 82.
174   Reynolds, *Saint John Fisher*, p. 82.
175   Ibid., p. 83.
176   Ibid., p. 83.
177   Roper, *The Mirrour of Vertue in Worldly Greatness or the Life of Sir Thomas More*), p. 298; Reynolds, *The Field is* Won, p. 298.
178   Roper, *The Mirrour of Vertue in Worldly Greatness or the Life of Sir Thomas More*, pp. 71–72.
179   Ibid., p. 72.
180   Moto Propio, Pope St. John Paul II, October 31, 2000; appendix.
181   Ibid., p. 52.
182   Ibid., pp. 53–54.
183   Ackroyd, *The Life of Thomas More,* p. 330.
184   Macklem, *God Have Mercy*, p. 61.
185   Ibid., pp. 32–33.
186   Vincent McNabb, *St.John Fisher* (Mediatrix Press, 1936), p. 30.
187   Reynolds, *Saint John Fisher*, p. 264.

Chapter 10: Injustice

188   Ackroyd, *A Daughter's Love*, p. 227.
189   Macklem, *God Have Mercy*, p. 177.
190   Ibid., p. 178.
191   Berger V U.S., 295 US 78, 888 (1935).

[192]   See e.g. Derrett, *The Trial of Sir Thomas More.*

[193]   Thomas More, *The History of King Richard the Third: A Reading Edition,* ed. George M. Logan (2005), p. 95.

[194]   This would not have worked with More, who said, "I never intend (God being my good lord) to pin my soul at another's back." Roper, *Life of Sir Thomas More,* p. 129.

[195]   Roper, *Life of Sir Thomas More,* p. 170.

[196]   Kelly, Karlin, Wegemer, *Thomas More's Trial by Jury,* p. 12.

Chapter 11: Malice

[197]   The words of the late H. Brent McKnight, judge of the Western District of North Carolina, at his judicial investiture, August 25, 2003 (transcript on file in Clerk's Office, WDNC).

[198]   Kelly, Karlin, Wegemer, *Thomas More's Trial by Jury,* p. 12.

[199]   Ibid., p. 111.

[200]   Ibid., p. 138.

[201]   Ibid., p. 168.

[202]   Ibid., p. 14.

[203]   "The courts must . . . lean in favor of a construction which will render every word operative, rather than one which may make some idle and nugatory." Thomas M. Cooley, quoted in Scalia and Garner, *Reading Law, The Interpretation of Legal Texts* (St Paul Minnesota: Thomson/West, 2012) chapter 26, Surplusage Canon, p. 174.

[204]   Reynolds, *Saint John Fisher,* pp. 277–78.

[205]   Ibid.

[206]   Ibid.

[207]   Kelly, Karlin, Wegemer, *Thomas More's Trial by Jury,* p. 205.

[208]   Ibid., p. 133.

[209]   Ibid., p. 200

[210]   Ibid., p. 196.

[211]   Bolt, *A Man for All Seasons,* p. 140–41.

Chapter 12: Condemned

[212]   Roper, *Life,* p. 165.

[213]   Macklem, *God Have Mercy,* p. 203.

[214]   Reynolds, *St. John Fisher,* pp. 279–80.

215   Ackroyd, *The Life of Thomas* More, p. 398.
216   Wegemer, Gerard, *Thomas More: A Portrait of Courage*, p. 192.
217   Macklem, *God Have Mercy*, p. 398. Ackroyd, *The Life of Thomas More*, p. 398.
218   St. John Paul II, *Apostolic Letter, Issued Motu Proprio, Proclaiming Saint Thomas More Patron of Statesmen and Politicians*, given at Saint Peters on October 31, 2000.
219   Ackroyd, *The Life of Thomas More*, pp. 405–6.
220   Reynolds, *The Field is Won*, p. 200.
221   Macklem, *God Have Mercy*, pp. 204–5.
222   Ibid., p. 205.
223   "So was I speaking and weeping in the most bitter contrition of my heart, when, lo! I heard from a neighboring house a voice, as of boy or girl, I know not, chanting, and oft repeating. 'Take up and read; Take up and read.' ['Tolle, lege! Tolle, lege!'] . . . Eagerly then I returned to the place where Alypius was sitting; for there had I laid the volume of the Apostle when I arose thence. I seized, opened, and in silence read that section on which my eyes first fell: 'Not in rioting and drunkenness, not in chambering and wantonness, not in strife and envying; but put ye on the Lord Jesus Christ, and make not provision for the flesh, in concupiscence.'" [Romans 13:14-15]. J. G. Pilkington, translator, *The Confessions of St. Augustine* (Norwalk: The Heritage Press, 1963), p. 141.
224   According to More, who told Meg: "I verily trust in God. He shall rather strengthen me to bear the loss, than against this conscience to swear and put my soul in peril." Roper, *Life of Sir Thomas More*, p. 143; Macklem, *God Have Mercy* , p. 205.
225   Ibid., p. 206.
226   Appendix.
227   O God, we praise Thee, and acknowledge Thee to be the supreme Lord.
      Everlasting Father, all the earth worships Thee.
      All the Angels, the heavens and all angelic powers,
      All the Cherubim and Seraphim, continuously cry to Thee:
      Holy, Holy, Holy, Lord God of Hosts!
      Heaven and earth are full of the Majesty of Thy glory.
      The glorious choir of the Apostles,
      The wonderful company of Prophets,
      The white-robed army of Martyrs, praise Thee.
      Holy Church throughout the world acknowledges Thee:

The Father of infinite Majesty;
Thy adorable, true and only Son;
Also the Holy Spirit, the Comforter.
O Christ, Thou art the King of glory!
Thou art the everlasting Son of the Father.
When Thou tookest it upon Thyself to deliver man,
Thou didst not disdain the Virgin's womb.
Having overcome the sting of death, Thou opened the Kingdom
of Heaven to all believers.
Thou sittest at the right hand of God in the glory of the Father.
We believe that Thou willst come to be our Judge.
We, therefore, beg Thee to help Thy servants whom Thou hast
redeemed with Thy Precious Blood.
Let them be numbered with Thy Saints in everlasting glory.

[228] Nichols, *St. John Fisher*, p. 20; McNabb, *St. John Fisher*, p. 129
[229] Late Middle English: from Old French parbouillir, from late Latin perbullire 'boil thoroughly,' from Latin per- 'through, thoroughly' (later confused with part) + bullire 'to boil.'
[230] Wegemer, Gerard, *Portrait of Courage*, p. 161.
[231] Roper, *The Mirrour of Vertue in Worldly Greatness or the Life of Sir Thomas More*, pp. 145, 169.

Appendix

[232] This prayer, without title, was written in the margins of More's prayer book while he was imprisoned in the Tower of London. See volume 13 of *The Complete Works of St. Thomas More* (Yale UP, 1976), pp. 226–27; *The Thomas More Source Book*, pp. 171–74; see also Thomasmorestudies.org/library/.
[233] thomasmorestudies.org/library/.

Bibliography

Ackroyd, Peter. *The Life of Thomas More*. New York: Nan A. Talese, 1998.

———. *Tudors: The History of England from Henry VIII to Elizabeth I*. New York: Thomas Dunne Books, 2012.

Basset, Bernard. *Born For Friendship: The Spirit of Thomas More*. Sheed and Ward, 1965.

Belloc, Hilaire. *Characters of the Reformation*. San Francisco: Ignatius Press, 2017.

Bolt, Robert. *A Man for All Seasons: A Play in Two Acts*. New York: Vintage Books, 1962.

Bradshaw, Brendan, and Duffy, Eamon, Eds. *Humanism, Reform and the Reformation: The Career of Bishop John Fisher Cambridge*. Cambridge University Press, 1989.

Brown and Curnow, *Tower of London*. London: Her Majesty's Stationery Office, 1984.

Campbell, W. E. *Erasmus, Tyndale and More*. The Bruce Publishing Company.

Curtwright, Travis, Ed. *Thomas More*. Lexington Books, 2015.

Daniel-Rops, H., *The Protestant Reformation*. London: J. M. Dent & Sons, 1962.

Davies, Michael. *Saint John Fisher: The Martyrdom of John Fisher, Bishop, During the Reign of King Henry VIII*. Long Prairie: The Neumann Press, 1988.

Dowling, Maria. *Fisher of Men: a Life of John Fisher*. MacMillan Press, 1999.

Farrow, John. *The Story of Thomas More*. New York: Sheed and Ward, 1954.

Guy, John. *A Daughter's Love, Thomas More & His Dearest Meg*. Houghton Mifflin Harcourt, 2009.

———. *Thomas More*. London, Arnold, 2000.

Hollis, Christopher. *Thomas More*. The Bruce Publishing Company, 1934.

Kelly, Karlin, and Wegemer. *Thomas More's Trial by Jury*. The Boydell Press, 2011.

MacCulloch, Diarmaid. *Thomas Cromwell: A Revolutionary Life*. New York: Viking, 2018.

Macklem, Michael. *God Have Mercy: The Life of John Fisher of Rochester*. Ottawa: Oberon Press, 1969.

McNabb, Vincent, *St. John Fisher*. Mediatrix Press, 1936.

Monti, James, *The King's Good Servant but God's First*. San Francisco: Ignatius Press, 1977.

More, Thomas. *Dialogue Concerning Heresies*. Ed. Mary Gotschalk. Princeton: Scepter Publishers, 2006.

———. *The Complete Works of St. Thomas More, Volume II, The History of King Richard III*. New Haven: Yale University Press, 1963.

Newman, John Henry. *Apologia Pro Vita Sua.* London: Longmans Green & Co, 1897.

———. *Certain Difficulties Felt by Anglicans in Catholic Teachings.* London: Longmans, Green, and Co., 1896.

———. *Loss and Gain.* Longmans Green & Co, 1898.

Nichols, Vincent. *St John Fisher: Bishop and Theologian in Reformation and Controversy.* Stoke-On-Trent: Alive Publishing, 2011.

Pilkington, J. G. translator. *The Confessions of St. Augustine.* Norwalk: The Heritage Press, 1963.

Reynolds, E .E. *The Field is Won: The Life and Death of Saint Thomas More.* Milwaukee: The Bruce Publishing Company, 1968.

———. *Margaret Roper: The Eldest Daughter of St. Thomas More.* New York: P. J. Kenedy & Sons.

———. *Saint John Fisher.* New York: P. J. Kenedy & Sons.

Roper, William. *The Mirrour of Vertue in Worldly Greatness or the Life of Sir Thomas More.* San Francisco: Ignatius Press, 2002.

Roper, William and Nicholas Harpsfield. *Lives of Saint Thomas More.* London: J. M. Dent & Sons, 1963.

Sargent, Daniel. *Thomas More.* Sheed & Ward, 1933.

Scalia, Antonin and Bryan A. Garner. *Reading Law: The Interpretation of Legal Texts.* St Paul Minnesota: Thomson/West, 2012.

Wegemer, Gerard B. *Thomas More: A Portrait of Courage.* Princeton: Scepter Publishers, 1998.

Wegemer, Gerard B. and Steven W. Smith, Eds. *A Thomas More Source Book.* The Catholic University of America Press, 2004.

Wegemer Gerard B., and Stephen W. Smith. *The Essential Works of Thomas More.* Yale University Press, 2020.